Book Cover Artist
Jan Frederik Kohler

FREE WILL
VS
PREDESTINATION

—— ❧ ——

*Does God know your choices
before you make them?*

THEODORE R. JOHNSTONE, M. D.

Order this book online at www.trafford.com
or email orders@trafford.com

Most Trafford titles are also available at major online book retailers.

Print information available on the last page.

ISBN: 978-1-4907-9488-4 (sc)
ISBN: 978-1-4907-9489-1 (e)

Library of Congress Control Number: 2019940798

Trafford rev. 07/03/2019

www.trafford.com
North America & international
toll-free: 1 888 232 4444 (USA & Canada)
fax: 812 355 4082

Contents

Preface

From the outset, Christianity has had to survive multiple man made divisions. The first one developed among the followers of Jesus soon after His ascension. At its center was the question of whether a non-Jewish person, who wanted to become a Christian, should be required to follow Jewish laws and customs. Not the least among these Jewish requirements, was whether or not gentile men should be circumcised. After a debate of early Church leaders led by Peter, it was decided that gentiles would not be required to follow most Jewish customs and laws, one of which was circumcision. (See Acts 15.) With this decision in place, Christianity gradually spread over most of Europe and Asia Minor.

Then in 1054 A.D., the eastern section of Christianity broke away from the western section forming what became known as the Eastern Orthodox Church. This left the mostly European division to become known as the Catholic, or universal Church. About 500 years after this geographic divide, the Reformation arose, led by Martin Luther. It split Christianity into two groups, the Catholics and the Protestants.

Next, about three decades after Luther, John Calvin came along as part of the Reformation, expounding the doctrine of Double Predestination. According to Calvin, God lives in an eternal "now" which allows Him to simultaneously see the past, present, and future, as in one continuous metaphorical sweep. Therefore God, in the beginning, could look ahead and actually create and predestine each person to eternal life or eternal damnation. This concept has divided Protestantism into two groups; those who believe the Bible teaches that each person's Free Will equips them to choose whether or not they want to become Christians or those who believe God has predestined each individual to their eternal destination, even before they were born. Calvin based this doctrine of Double Predestination, mainly on his interpretation of Ephesians chapter one and Romans chapter eight. These scriptures, along with others, are analyzed in this book.

One of the reasons for writing of this little five-chapter book occurred as a result of seeing the doctrine of Predestination divide the church that my wife and I attend. We saw the problems this doctrine caused among otherwise solid believing Protestant Christians. It ended with the congregation splitting, when two of the five pastors led about three hundred people to leave our congregation of around 3,000 and form another church. Fortunately, for both sides, very little, if any animosity existed then or now about the separation. This undoubtedly was due to the way the head pastor handled the situation; plus the fact that the group that split off were given a six-figure amount of money to start up their new church.

In dialogue form, this book takes up the supposed experiences of a group of make believe modern day Christians as they explore the problems that arise when they compare and contrast Free Will with Predestination. Chapter one deals with God's "dilemma" at the time of creation, as to how He would equip intelligent creatures to choose or not to choose. Chapter two lays out Biblical definitions needed to better understand the differences between the doctrines of Free Will and Predestination. Chapters three, four, and five, respectively, take up problems of interpretation, which are encountered with these two doctrines, as found in Ephesians and Romans, prophecies in general, and various divisions of science.

Theodore R. Johnstone, M.D.

Chapter One

Man's Free Will and God's Sovereignty

Many devout Christians and their clergy rarely consider the effects that would accrue on God's **omniscience**, all knowing (see 1 John 3:20), and **omnipotence**, all powerful (see Genesis 17:1), if God decided to give all intelligent creatures the ability to make independent, uncoerced, freewill choices before they were created. However, two questions regarding this decision beg to be answered:

1. When intelligent creatures were created, either angelic or human, did God choose to allow them to make independent, uncoerced, freewill choices, not under His sovereignty, in order to give them freedom to choose?
2. Would all their choices need to be unknowable to God until after they were made to guarantee that Deity could not be accused of originating the evil?

If God could create the universe, then He certainly would have possessed **omniscience** and **omnipotence**, meaning that He had infinite knowledge and power. Therefore God, if He wanted, would have had both all the knowledge and power needed to create intelligent creatures with choosing mechanisms, the choices of which He could not know until after they were made. Any contrary notion would place a limitation on what God would have been able to create. From a human perspective, an increase in knowledge frequently has a direct, positive effect on power, indicating that an increase in knowledge often produces an increase in power. As an example, with increased knowledge of the atom, physicists learned how to tap into the energy of the atomic nucleus. With this

1

knowledge, they soon produced the atomic bomb and the release of its huge power. However, before creation, God's **omniscience** and **omnipotence** were already infinite, **so** the simultaneous use of them would have resulted in a perfect creation.

A Divine Revelation

Now imagine the discussions and conclusions that would emerge from a make-believe group of modern-day Christians, if via an imaginary simultaneous Divine Revelation to each one in the group, God reenacted the last part of the sixth creation day in their collective presence. Suppose, in all of God's **omniscience** and **omnipotence**, the group was shown, during three successive episodes, how Adam and Eve had been made in God's image and three different but possible ways God could have equipped them to make choices regarding good and evil. But during each reenactment, keep in mind that if good or evil existed, both would have been powerless concepts bereft of an intelligent mind able to notice the differences and choose between the two. Then afterward, suppose that God made it possible for this group of Christians to observe what would have happened over time, if He had taken various routes with respect to how Adam and Eve had been equipped to choose.

But don't forget that human goodness from God's perspective always equates with unconditional love and unselfishness, both of which can be demonstrated by how we choose to place others. Goodness always chooses to place the other person first and itself last. Whereas, evil always is based on choosing to place oneself first and others last. In fact, when you violate any of the Ten Commandments, you inadvertently are placing yourself either above God or people. Breaking any of the first four places you above God and the violating any of last six attempts to elevate you above your fellow man. Placing yourself above someone else is a selfish act, which makes selfishness a disguised form of disrespect for the other person and usually has destructive effects on both the perpetrator and on the one to whom the selfishness is directed.

However, during each of the proposed reenactments, two questions should arise in the minds of this imaginary group of modern-day Christians: (1) Was disbelief in God coupled with selfish pride the root of Adam and Eve's original sin in the garden? (2) Is disbelief in God and selfish pride the foundation of every sinful choice that humans ever have made?

Each of the three reveled episodes that follow will show what might have occurred in the afternoon on day six of creation and for a time afterward.

Episode I

What would have happened if God had placed a restriction in the brains of Adam and Eve that would have prevented them from making any selfish choice rooted in pride? Keep in mind that even if their brains had not been pre-fixed, making it impossible to choose anything selfish, it would have been difficult for them to make wrong choices in the Garden of Eden anyway. Just think, atheism would have been ruled out every time God visited them in the cool of the day. Neither had earthly parents, whom they could dishonor. There would have been no one else but themselves to murder and no one with whom to commit adultery. In this environment, from whom could either of them steal or covet? To whom could they lie? In fact, a whole row of Trees of Knowledge of Good and Evil should not have tested their loyalty to God in the slightest.

Keep in mind that this Christian group watched Episode I while under a generalized epiphany. They noticed that Adam and Eve, whose brains were equipped with a limiting mechanism, made it impossible for them to choose prideful selfishness and evil. Therefore, these modern-day Christian observers were struck by the perfect unselfish living, demonstrated by this primordial pair. Since everyone in this group had experienced prideful selfish evil in their modern-day lives, they were forced to conclude that God had not chosen to place any restrictive mechanism in the human brain.

Episode II

Next, contemplate, if, under similar conditions, God had allowed the Christian onlookers to see what would have happened if no restriction had been inserted into the brains of Adam and Eve. Instead, in this situation, the newly created pair would be allowed to make independent, uncoerced, freewill choices, not under God's sovereignty, as long as every choice was **foreknown** to Him prior to its occurrence.

Having found that the restriction presented in Episode I had produced results that did not agree with their experience, this group of Christian observers became somewhat reluctant to accept this new condition until it could be tested against what they knew to be real in their modern-day lives.

In spite of the hesitation, one of the observers, Dave, said, "This seems more like our everyday earthly experience. We intuitively know we can choose whatever we want at any time we want, and since God is supposed to be in charge of the future, what difference would it make if He knows ahead of time every choice we humans are going to make?"

Bill, with a deep penetrating voice, then interjected. "What I have trouble getting a handle on is this: If God created all intelligent creatures with the freedom to choose anything and if He knew in advance what each person's choice was going to be, even before the person was created, then every choice would have been prefixed in His omniscient mind."

"So what?" Gary emphatically inserted. "We make good and bad choices every day. These prove that God made us so we can make free-will choices. Tell me then, what would be wrong with His having prior knowledge with respect to every good or selfish choice we make?"

Turning to Gary, Bill replied, "Well, the problem is this: If God knew in advance who was going to make the first selfish choice before He even created that person, and if He went ahead creating him anyway, then knowingly, God would become responsible for having created the first evil anywhere in the universe."

"God wouldn't really create any evil, would He?" Gayle questioned.

"No, He wouldn't, Gayle. That's why God could have used His foreknowledge to prevent any evil from contaminating this terrestrial globe," Linda observed.

"Well, He didn't use His foreknowledge to prevent evil on this earth," Annie said emphatically, "because we see it everywhere we look. I've seen plenty of it in my life."

With a slow drawl, Ted pointed out, "The only way God could give us free will without being the inevitable originator of evil would be by creating us so He could not know what any choice was going to be until after it was made."

Karen, who had been listening intently, interrupted. "How could God not know what choices we are going to make when He can read our minds?"

"That's right," Barbara commented. "Unless God created us so He could read our minds up to just before we chose, and then He wouldn't know for sure what choice we were going to make until after we made it."

With that comment, there was silence for a few seconds as each person thought it over.

"I hate arguments about theological topics," Loran said quietly. "So why don't we just watch what God is doing right now in this present reenactment? Maybe we can learn something."

"Yes, I see what's happened," Janice, the leader of the group, noted. "We got so involved in our suppositions that we took our eyes off God's second reenactment. Perhaps we should consider the quality of His work and not argue about the subject matter."

When they looked, all were surprised to see that God had already abandoned Episode II and had started the next one. Obviously, He didn't want to use any part of His foreknowledge to condemn Himself.

Episode III

However, before the group could return to the basics of watching God in the third reenactment of human creation, Lee, one of the observers who frequently arrived late, entered just in time to hear the last part of the conversation. Thinking he had an answer to the dilemma in which the group seemed to be caught, he said loudly, "Let me tell you what John Calvin, one of the early Christian Reformers, taught."

"Oh no!" shouted Bill and Dave simultaneously. "We're Catholics."

"It won't hurt you to look at the other side of this metaphorical theological coin, so bear with me for just a minute," Lee retorted.

"Okay, just for a minute."

"Calvin believed, from his study of two New Testament texts, the first in Romans 8:28–30 and the second in Ephesians 1:1–14, that God Himself, by His foreknowledge, determined in the beginning, before the creation of the world, that He would predestine some humans for eternal life and others for damnation. I just happen to have a quote of his right here in my smart phone. Give me a sec, and I'll pull it up."

As he hunted for it, Lee kept on talking. "John Calvin, a Frenchman, wrote this statement, along with many others, while living in Basel, Switzerland. (Later, he moved to Geneva.) He, with several others, led in the reformation against the teachings of the Roman Catholic Church. Ah, here's his quote:

> When we attribute foreknowledge to God, we mean that everything has always been and forever remains in his full view, so in terms of his knowledge, there is nothing which is either future or past . . . We call predestination God's eternal counsel by which he has determined what he wishes to do with each and every person. For he does not create them all in like condition but appoints some to eternal life and others to eternal damnation. Thus, according to the end for which a person has been created, we say that he is predestined to death or life."[1]

"According to Calvin's interpretation of these texts," Lee continued, "the destiny of all humans has been predetermined before the foundation of the world by divine fiat. Therefore, humans have no choice in their eternal outcome. Three other New Testament texts are often cited to bolster this theological doctrine of double predestination. They are Romans 11:2–4, 1 Peter 1:1–2, and Acts 2:23 (all NIV), where words such as 'foreknew' and 'foreknowledge' are found. These also indicate that God knows in advance what choices humans are going to make."

"This is heretical!" Ted yelled out. "It indicates that God capriciously has chosen each person's eternal destiny before their creation, maybe half of them good and half evil."

"You mean to tell me, Lee, some Christians believe this stuff?" questioned Tom, who was new to the group.

Before Lee could answer, Ted inserted, "Yes, sadly, millions do. It's because they take what the clergy tells them without reading the Bible or thinking things out for themselves. If the above were true, evangelism would be worthless because everyone's eternal destiny would have been predetermined by a deity, who randomly chose to create some of us with desirable outcomes and others for, well, you know what. In addition, by pronouncing everything good at the end of day six, God would have lied if He just had created someone to be damned. Worst of all, if God had created some intelligent beings predestined for damnation, He would have denied the existence of His unconditional love for everyone.[2] If this concept is true, then there could be no such thing as a 'rebel' because God would have chosen to create some people as 'rebels.' A decision like that would have made it impossible for any 'rebel' to 'repent' and receive forgiveness. So why would it be necessary for Jesus to die to save sinners who could never be lost or die to clean up the mess that supposedly God the Father had caused in the first place? In these circumstances, mercy and grace could not be involved in anyone's salvation? Many Christians don't realize that when God created intelligent creatures, He gave them the ability to make free will choices for a reason."

"And what could that possibly be?" asked Kathy.

With that question, everyone was quiet again for a few seconds, so Loran, right on cue, said, "Let's look at what's happening in Episode III."

The group turned their attention just in time to see God put the final touches on a clay model of what looked like a man that was soon to be Adam. Then God "breathed into his nostrils the breath of life," and the lump of clay "became a living being." Then God gave Adam the responsibility of naming the fish, birds, and animals, over which he was to rule, and placed him in the garden, for which he was to care. Next, God anesthetized him and took one of his ribs, from which He created Eve. Then God brought the woman to the man. They both were naked. The first thing Adam saw, while recovering from God's anesthesia, was Eve's beautiful face.

Suddenly, all eyes of the group became riveted on the scene.

"Look at the expression on Adam's face!" exclaimed Carole. "He can't believe his eyes."

"Their faces seem full of wonder, and neither one appears to be ashamed," Hans pointed out.

Then Bob exclaimed, "Look! Adam's trying to stand up, and Eve is helping him."

The observations soon became self-sustaining with different ones participating all at once.

"Now they're just standing there trying to size each other up."

"Look! Adam's taking hold of her right hand with his left."

"And Eve has put her left hand around Adam's waist."

"Adam, with his right hand, is taking hold of Eve's chin, turning her head up a little as he leans over for his first kiss."

"Oh, Adam is such a lover. I can't imagine what Eve's thinking." Gayle sighed.

"You dummy!" Pat exclaimed. "I know what she's thinking. 'Be fruitful and multiply.'"

"This is too taxing for me," muttered John.

"They're making a lot of good free will choices right before our eyes," Janice noted. "But don't forget it was God who created husbands and wives to act this way, and He was nearby watching. I wonder, however, what choices they'll make if confronted with an actual temptation to be selfish?"

That situation wasn't long in coming. Perhaps one day Eve wandered a short distance from Adam's side and found herself adjacent to the Tree of Knowledge of Good and Evil. A beautiful talking snake was up in the tree.

It said, "Did God tell you not to eat the fruit from this tree?"

"Yes," she replied. "If we do, we will die."

"You won't die. I didn't, and see, now I can talk. You're smarter than me, so if you eat it, you will be like God, knowing good and evil."

"When the woman saw that the fruit of the tree was good for food and pleasing to the eye, and also desirable for gaining wisdom, she took some and ate it. She also gave some to her husband, who was with her, and he ate it." (Genesis 3:1–7)

Eve thought, *God told us we'd die if we ate the fruit. The serpent said we wouldn't. Also, if I ate it, I'd be as smart as God.* So she chose to believe the serpent instead of God, thus ended the imaginary simultaneous Divine Revelation of this group of modern-day Christians.

Discussions Resulting from the Imaginary Divine Revelation Episodes

"This proves that God, at creation, gave mankind the ability to make independent, uncoerced, freewill choices, but how could He do this without condemning Himself, and why?" Hank asked.

"And that's what I want to know," iterated Kathy.

"Before we find out why God granted humans free will," Ted said, "we need to find out how He could do this without self-condemnation. From what happened at the end of Episode III and what we experience each day of our lives, we intuitively know that we can make independent, uncoerced, freewill choices. But the only way God could give us this option is by granting us a generalized permit to make choices without His immediate permission. This situation would require Him to share with us small portions of His **omnipotence** (power) and **omniscience** (knowledge). His **omnipotence** is shared with us every time we make a free will choice without His prior permission. God also shares a little of His **omniscience** with us any time we make a free will choice without His knowing about it first."

"Would God share any of His **omnipotence** and **omniscience** with humans?" asked Howard.

"Well, He already has," Phillip said emphatically. "Creation of new life is the supreme evidence that God possesses both **omnipotence** and **omniscience**. Yet procreation of new life is something He has shared with humans and all carbon-based life but not with angels. (See Matthew 22:30.) Humans possess intelligence, but many forms of earthly life have none at all. We humans don't have to get permission from God to procreate. In fact, He has commanded us, along with all other earthly creatures, to 'be fruitful and increase in number, fill the earth.' Therefore, this command requires Him to share some of His **omnipotence** (power) and **omniscience** (knowledge) with us."

A few subdued snickers followed Phillip's observation. So Ted, with an obvious grin, quickly took up the slack by saying. "Great point, Phillip, but let me give you an analogy similar to how God might share some of His **omnipotence** (Psalm 68:35) and **omniscience** (Psalm 119:66) with us. Perhaps this situation would be like Bill Gates giving someone a dollar. If we let his billions represent his total economic power, then his choice to donate a buck would have diminished his wealth by only a dollar. But basically, his economic power would not have changed at all. Before the donation, he controlled how every cent of his fortune would be spent, but afterward, he lost control not only of the one hundred pennies he had donated, but also the foreknowledge of how the recipient was going use them until after they were spent. The recipient was free to spend the money any way he chose.

"To most people, Bill Gates' huge wealth may seem almost infinite, but it is finite. However, God's **omnipotence** and **omniscience** are both infinite. Therefore, if God decided to give His intelligent creatures permission to make freewill choices independent of His sovereignty and knowledge, His sharing of a miniscule portion of these entities would be infinitely smaller than the fraction a dollar would make if divided by Bill Gates' huge fortune. Therefore, God gives up none of His strength and knowledge when He shares some of each with us."

"This makes sense," Phyllis interrupted. "I can understand how God could make a person's choices not be under His immediate authority because if He gave everyone permission to choose without His prior permission, then every choice still would be with His permission. We could liken this to an army officer during the Civil War commanding his troops to fire at will. Each soldier could shoot his gun at the enemy as he saw fit. With his command, the captain shared a little of his authority and knowledge with every individual soldier by delegating to each one the responsibility of choosing at whom and when to shoot. However, the captain didn't lose any of his authority by giving this command. Before giving it, he trusted that each soldier's training had provided him with enough knowledge to choose appropriately before firing each shot. In fact, under these conditions, it would be unthinkable to shoot at a fellow trooper and not at the enemy.

"Likewise, before God gave any intelligent creature permission to choose at will, He also gave each one instructions on how to choose and what would happen if they chose wrong. He trusted, with His pre-choice instructions, that their intelligence would guide them correctly. Under these conditions, a selfish choice could be a possibility but not inevitable. If a selfish choice was made, however, the responsibility of making it would fall on the intelligent creature as the originator of evil and not on God the Creator."

"Great observation, Phyllis," Ted broke in, "but keep in mind what we learned earlier, how knowledge, with us humans, has a positive effect on our power, meaning an increase in knowledge produces an increase in power. But because God's knowledge has always been infinite, and therefore, **omniscient**, it could not increase His power at all because God's infinite knowledge automatically made Him all-powerful or **omnipotent**. Therefore, the only way that God's knowledge and power could ever be affected was if something new occurred in the universe that before had never been present. That something was overt selfishness first introduced into the heavenly universe by the choice of Lucifer, later known as Satan, when he said in his heart, 'I will make myself like the Most High.'" (Isaiah 14:14)

Ted continued. "Satan's wrong choice in heaven did not mean that God had not previously envisioned the repercussions that would accrue on Himself and all the created occupants of the universe, as well, if one of His intelligent creatures chose to be selfish. God also had anticipated the effects this choice would have on His **omniscience** and **omnipotence** and the cost required to correct it. God was not taken by surprise but was greatly disappointed by Satan's choice.

"Regardless, the practice of overt selfishness had never been present in the universe before Satan made his choice. It was something new, an all-out assault on the principles of unconditional love and unselfishness, which before this had always reigned by placing others first. Ezekiel, writing of Satan, says in chapter 28:15, 'You were blameless in your ways from the day you were created till wickedness was found in you.'

"Satan, by his choice, turned everything around in the opposite direction. He may have thought that if everyone places himself first and others last, a healthy competition might develop between various people, bringing out the best in each, like survival of the fittest. However, with the passage of thousands of years since humans chose to follow Satan's philosophy, his postulate has been proven wrong. The finding is that selfish pride always produces detrimental effects on the perpetrator and also on the one at whom it is directed. It is similar to a crazy Civil War soldier with a defective gun, shooting at will at fellow troopers. His gun not only discharges a bullet toward the one it is aimed, but also backfires on the shooter every time he pulls the trigger. Selfishness is like that. It has two ugly prongs, which eventually will produce the deaths of both the perpetrator and the other selfish person at whom the selfishness is directed."

Lee, who had listened without entering into the discussion, broke his silence again by saying, "Everything you folks have proposed will be void because it all depends on God not knowing what someone has chosen until after the person makes a choice. This notion is impossible when you consider that God can read each of our minds before we choose. That's why Calvin has to be right. Before God made us, He decided which way each one of us was going to choose, either good or evil. Therefore, each of our choices would be known to Him before we chose."

"Lee," Ted interrupted, "there's no question that God, being all knowing and all powerful, could have made intelligent creatures with minds He could read and predict their choices. But if He had done this, God, with His foreknowledge, would have known in advance the person making the first evil choice. Therefore, He created intelligent creatures with minds He could read except for their choices. Before we make freewill choices, neither God nor we can know what our choice is going to be until after it is made. In giving intelligent creatures freewill to choose without Him being able to predict their choices, God cannot be blamed for wittingly having created someone whom He could have known beforehand would introduce selfishness into the universe."

Barging into the discussion again, Gary spoke up. "And, Lee, if God could not know our choices ahead of time, this would ensure humans the complete freedom to choose. In this situation, He would share a little of His **omnipotence** with us every time we made an independent, free-will choice without His direct permission. He'd also share a little of His **omniscience** by learning what choice we made, which previously had been unknown to Him."

Loren, a math teacher, responded to Gary's comment. "**Omnipotence** and **omniscience** are both infinite, meaning they have no beginning or end. No number can be used to add, subtract, multiply, or divide with infinity. Therefore, it cannot be changed because no matter what you try to do to it, infinity stays the same. Regardless, most Christians would have difficulty even thinking of this, much less believing that God, who does not change, would share extremely small portions of His infinite knowledge and power with His intelligent creatures. But God had to share some with us for freewill choices to be available.

"Notwithstanding, this brief excursion into the infinite properties of God's knowledge and authority, He shared with humans something much greater than small portions of these two entities, when He gave us His Son. Not only did Jesus share some of His omniscience and omnipotence with us, but also a small amount of our mortality as well. He gave up His royal position in heaven to become encased in the very carbon-based life in which He had created us. Clothed in a human body allowed this divine person to share three days of death with us. Since He shares **omnipotence** and **omniscience** with God the Father, His death can cover the sins of all humanity among those who choose to believe God again. Believers, thereby, can share in His resurrection and receive everlasting life. All this was done to give back to mankind eternal life, which they had lost by misuse of their free will choices. God knew in advance, prior to creating intelligent creatures, the price the Trinity would have to pay to correct the entrance of selfish pride into the universe, if angels or humans, equipped to make free will choices, chose wrong."

"If angels, created with free will choice, who had been created perfect, had sinned in heaven, why would God repeat the situation all over again by creating humans with free will choice?" Ted asked.

"I realize what I'm about to say harks back to what was discussed earlier," Dave said, "but my first reaction to the proposal that God could create intelligent creatures whose decisions would remain unknowable to Him until after we make them seemed like nonsense. But now it doesn't seem ridiculous at all when we realize any contrary notion places a restriction on what God would have been able to create. Sometimes, however, when God reacts so quickly to our wrong choices, it seems like He foreknew what our choices were going to be before we make them."

Bill, the thinker, quickly responded. "We must look at these situations from God's perspective. When we are about to choose, God can see in advance every possible choice available to us and knows ahead of time what His best response will be for any given choice we decide to make. His rapid response, therefore, makes it look like He foreknew what each of our choices were going to be prior to our making them. God's rapid response, however, need not be dependent on His foreknowing what a given choice would be."

"Okay, fellas, I like your reasoning," Kathy blurted out, "but what I want to know is why God would give us free will in the first place if He could foresee that a lot of trouble would result if someone made one wrong choice."

"All right, Kathy, let's go there," Ted said. "Friendship and love for others should not depend totally on your feelings, but also should be subservient to your will. True love always involves giving up some of your freedom, autonomy, and independence. When you love anyone, at a minimum, a portion of your time must be devoted to them. Because you want to please the one you love, you must make choices that involve them as well as yourself. In short, since you don't know for sure how your loved one will accept your attempts at showing affection, you must be willing to place what you think you know about them on hold until you can see their response. You, thereby, have been willing, unwittingly, to place your knowledge and your power to choose subservient to your loved one until that person makes a response. Freedom to love someone always comes with the risk of being rejected. Your heart may be broken in the process. That's a chance you must take. However, when free will and feelings of both persons come together simultaneously, each obtains requited love.

"God's attempts to draw us back to Himself are no different. He shared a small portion of His knowledge (**omniscience**) and power to choose for us (**omnipotence**) when He gave us free will. And just as we wait to see the response of a loved one to our amorous attempts, so also God waits to see ours. But in the end, as it is with any successful love, the loss of freedom and independence that each one voluntarily gives to the relationship is more than made up when each one receives love in return. Without freewill choices, agape love could not proceed from God to us, or from us to God, or from us to others. Each person, including God, 'Who first loved us,' must be able to make freewill choices.[3] When God created intelligent creatures with free will, He took the same risk. He wanted to share His love with them and have them freely return love back to Him. A bilateral loving response is the most important reason God gave angels and humans free will. Without free will, agape love could not exist. Therefore, we can conclude that God knows everything about each one of us, except for the next choice we are going to make."

Just then, Annie, a devout Presbyterian, interrupted, exclaiming, "Okay, Ted, this analysis of man's free will and God's sovereignty is very interesting, but since my church was founded on Calvin's teachings, I want you to go over the New Testament texts that he used as a foundation for his teachings."

"I'll do just that, Annie, but the facial expression on Janice's face tells me that this explanation will have to wait till we meet next week as it is getting late."

With that, Janice dismissed the group by saying, "We'll take this up then."

Summary of Chapter One

1. God is **omniscient** (all knowing), 1 John 3:20.
2. God is **omnipotent** (all powerful), Geneses 17:1.
3. Therefore, God could create anything that He desired.
4. Placing any restriction on what God could create places a restriction on what God could know (**omniscience**) and on what God could create (**omnipotence**).
5. Many devout Christians and their clergy rarely consider the effects that would accrue on God's **omniscience** and **omnipotence** if He decided to give all intelligent creatures the ability to make independent, uncoerced, freewill choices before they were created.
6. Before creating a given intelligent being, either angelic or human, if God knew in advance that the being was going to sin, and if

He went ahead and created this being anyway, then God would be responsible for creating the first evil in the universe.

7. Therefore, in order for God to be able to create intelligent creatures and not be responsible for originating evil, He had to create them so that their choices would remain unknowable to Him until after they were made.

8. In order for God to create intelligent creatures having the ability to make independent, uncoerced, freewill choices unknowable to him would require Him to share small amounts of his **omniscience** and **omnipotence** with them as they were created.

9. Since God's **omniscience** and **omnipotence** are each infinite, it would be impossible to add anything to either one to make them bigger or subtract anything from either one make them smaller. Therefore, if God made creatures in His own image, by sharing small amounts of His **omniscience** or **omnipotence** with them, His **omniscience** and **omnipotence** would not change at all. Each would remain infinite.

10. Keep in mind, human goodness from God's perspective always equates with unconditional love and unselfishness, both of which can be demonstrated by how we choose to place others. Goodness always chooses to place the other person first and itself last.

11. So why would God want to create intelligent creatures who could make independent, uncoerced, freewill choices in the first place if He could foresee that a lot of trouble would result if any one of them made one selfish choice?

12. Love for others should not depend totally on your feelings, but also should be subservient to your will. True love always involves giving up some of your freedom, autonomy, and independence. When you love someone, at a minimum, a portion of your time must be devoted to them. Because you want to please the one you love, you must make choices that involve them as well as yourself.

13. In short, since you don't know for sure how your loved one will accept your attempts at showing affection, you must be willing to place what you think you know about them on hold until you can see their response.

14. You, thereby, have been willing, unwittingly, to place your knowledge and your power to choose, subservient to your loved one until that person makes a response. Freedom to love someone

always comes with the risk of being rejected. Your heart may be broken in the process. That's the chance you must take. However, when free will and feelings of both persons come together simultaneously, each obtains requited love.

15. "God's attempts to draw us back to Himself are no different. He shared a small portion of His knowledge (**omniscience**) and power to choose for us (**omnipotence**) when He gave us free-will. And just as we wait to see the response of a loved one to our amorous attempts, so also God waits to see ours. But in the end, as it is with any successful love, the loss of freedom and independence that each one voluntarily gives to the relationship is more than made up when each one receives love in return.

16. Without freewill choices, agape love could not proceed from God to us, or from us to God, or from us to other humans. Each person, including God, "Who first loved us," must be able to make freewill choices.[3] When God created intelligent creatures with freewill, He took the same risk. He wanted to share His love with them and have them freely return love back to Him.

17. A bilateral loving response is the most important reason God gave angels and humans free will. Without free will, agape love could not exist. <u>Therefore, we can conclude that God knows everything about each one of us, except for the next choice we are going to make.</u>

18. Therefore, the only way that God's knowledge and power could ever have been affected was if something new occurred in the universe that never had been present before. That something was overt selfishness, first introduced into the heavenly universe by the choice of Lucifer, later known as Satan, when he said in his heart, "I will make myself like the Most High." (Isaiah 14:14)

The So-Called Doctrine of Predestination

19. The doctrine of predestination was taught by Calvin, one of the early Christian Reformers. This teaching places nearly everything described in items 20–22 in question. One quotation of Calvin's will be cited as an example: "When we attribute foreknowledge to God, we mean that everything has always been and forever remains, in his full view, so, in terms of his knowledge, there is nothing which is either future or past . . . We call predestination

God's eternal counsel by which he has determined what he wishes to do with each and every person. For He does not create them all in like condition, but appoints some to eternal life and others to eternal damnation. Thus, according to the end for which a person has been created, we say that he is predestined to death or to life."[1]

20. Calvin came up with the doctrine of double predestination, based mainly on his misinterpretation of two Bible texts found in Ephesians 1:1–14 and Romans 8:28–30. These two texts were supplemented with several others found in Romans 11:2–4, 1 Peter 1:1–2, and Acts 2:23 (all NIV), where words such as "foreknew" and "foreknowledge" are found. These texts seem to indicate that God knows in advance what choices humans are going to make.

21. However, if God, before creating each intelligent being, either angelic or human, had decided in advance by divine fiat to create some for eternal life and others for damnation, then God would be responsible for willfully creating the first evil in the universe.

22. If the doctrine of double predestination is true, it would make evangelism useless, since everybody's eternal destiny would have been predetermined by divine fiat and not by forgiveness of sin derived from the life, death, and resurrection of Jesus. Why would Jesus have to die to clean up a mess that God the Father had caused by His precreation choices in the first place?

Bibliography

1. Calvin, John. *Institutes of the Christian Religion*, pp. 466–467. Translated from the first French edition of 1541 by Robert White 2014. The Banner of Truth Trust. PO Box 621, Carlisle, Pennsylvania 17013, USA.
2. Gallemore, Tim. A suggestion made by him on May 25, 2012.
3. Keller, Timothy. *The Reason for God,* pp. 48-50, 2008. Penguin Group. New York, New York.

Chapter Two

Man's Free Will and God's Sovereignty (Part Two)

---- ⌘ ----

A week later, when this same make-believe group of Christians met, everyone seemed anxious to see Ted's reaction to Lee's expounding of Calvin's teaching and the relationship between man's free will and God's sovereignty.

Janice had some difficulty bringing the meeting to order because of the conversations going on among the group about the topic. When she finally succeeded, she asked Lee to open with prayer. He agreed and prayed for the Holy Spirit to bring understanding and unity to their study of scripture.

After Lee's "Amen," Janice immediately said, "All right, Ted, give us those New Testament texts that John Calvin used to substantiate his so-called doctrine of double predestination and how you differ from his interpretation and why. It's called double predestination because, as Lee read to us last week, some people are predestined to eternal life and some to perdition. You know, Ted, that Calvin's Bible teachings have been around for hundreds of years, so we are very interested to know how your understanding of this subject differs from his."

"Great observation, Janice," Ted responded, "but before going directly to the texts that Calvin used, we need to obtain a Biblical definition of several words or terms to understand the famous texts that Calvin used."

Annie broke in at this point by reminding everyone that it was her question the week before that had prompted this discussion. "So, Ted," she said, "I'm all ears. What Biblical definitions do you have in mind?"

"Well, Annie, I'm thinking of God's <u>mercy</u> and His <u>grace,</u> God's <u>elect</u> and His <u>election,</u> God's <u>purpose</u> and His <u>call</u> and His <u>justification</u>." Turning to Hans, Ted asked, "How would you define God's mercy?"

With a questioning look on his face and after thinking for a moment, he said, "I believe it's God's postponement of dispensing a deserved but inevitable and undesirable outcome, namely death."

"Lee, do you agree?" Ted questioned. "And can you cite a Bible text that upholds that definition?"

"I'll buy that meaning," Lee retorted. "But I can't cite any biblical text."

"May I give you some suggestions?"

Smirking, he said, "Sure, Ted, I'll take help from whomever I can get it, even from you."

When the laughing subsided, Ted proceeded. "Okay, Lee. God told Adam in the garden, before creating Eve (Genesis 2:15–17), that if he ate the fruit from the Tree of Knowledge of Good and Evil, he would die. Later, these two, using their free will, chose to believe Satan instead of God. Satan had said they wouldn't die if they ate the forbidden fruit, and in addition, he implied that they would 'be like God, knowing good and evil.' (Genesis 3:4) Eating some fruit has no moral implication. The wrongness of their act came from believing Satan instead of God. Satan said they wouldn't die if they ate it and their status would be elevated to that of God's. Together, Adam and Eve brought death on the entire human race with their selfish choice, but God, in His mercy, postponed their death for a time until they learned to believe Him. Micah 7:18–19 tells us that God 'pardons sin and forgives the transgression' and also takes delight in showing mercy. Paul says in Ephesians 2:4, 'But because of His love for us, God, who is rich in mercy made us alive in Christ even when we were dead in transgressions.' Romans 11:32 says, 'For God has bound all men over to disobedience so that he may have mercy on them all.'

"Adam and Eve chose to disbelieve God when He said that death would result from eating the forbidden fruit. He didn't say that He would kill them if they ate it. He only said that they would die if they ate it. God said nothing about giving them an eternal punishment in Hell if they ate it. By believing Satan instead of God, we, like Adam and Eve, in effect, are saying that God lied when He told them that eating the fruit would result in death. We are saying that we know better than

God and trying to make ourselves equal to Him or even better with our disbelief. The death that all mankind has experienced ever since the primordial pair ate the fruit in the garden is the inevitable result of disbelieving God combined with an act of selfish pride. Therefore, death is not a punishment from God because of disobedience. Mercy is the time God grants us before this earthly life ends to change our minds and make the unselfish choice to believe Him instead of Satan. Eternal death is the inevitable result of our persistence in selfish disbelief. So you see, Hans was right when he told us that mercy is a postponement of receiving a deserved but inevitable and undesirable outcome, namely death. It is the inevitable result of our disbelieving God and our attempt at self-aggrandizement.

"Now let's try to define the Biblical meaning of God's grace." Pointing to Dave, Ted asked, "Can you give us a definition of God's grace?"

"I'm no theologian, but from what we've just learned about mercy, I'd guess His grace has to be the opposite of His mercy, which would mean getting a reward we don't deserve."

"That's great, Dave," Ted said. "So can anyone recite a Biblical text with this definition?"

Several hands went up at the same time, but Gayle shouted out, "Ephesians 2:8–9: 'For it is by grace you have been saved, through faith—and this is not from yourselves, it is the gift of God—not by works, so that no one can boast.'"

"From what are we supposedly being saved, and when does this happen?" questioned Linda.

"Eternal death," Hans blurted, "and this happens when anyone places their faith or belief in Jesus instead of Satan. In fact, the only unpardonable sin occurs when we persist in believing Satan instead of God. Satan's postulates hold selfishness to be the best way to live. This notion is opposed to God's axiom of complete unselfishness. Ultimately though, the believer gets the undeserved reward at the second coming of Jesus, when He restores eternal life to those who believe Him."

"And, Hans, from what Bible texts was this information obtained?" Ted asked.

"Well, Ted, John 3:16 states that whosoever believes in Jesus will not perish, and Matthew 25:31–46 tells us that this finally occurs at the return of Jesus."

"Good, Hans. From man's perspective, however, God's mercy had to come first. If it hadn't, we would all have died immediately after sinning because 'we all have sinned.' (Romans 3:23) God, by His mercy, postponed our death so that He can save us by the gift of His grace through faith, which is simply believing in Jesus."

"I never thought of this before," Karen mumbled aloud. "God's mercy actually does have to precede His grace, doesn't it?"

"Yes, it does, Karen."

Gary then asked, "Ted, does everyone get God's mercy, followed by His grace?"

"Yes, Gary, everyone gets God's mercy, even before they choose to believe in Jesus. But after anyone chooses to believe and repent, God will dispense His grace on that individual and forgive that person's sins. His grace entitles them to eternal life. However, those who refuse to believe in Jesus get little or no grace but mainly mercy until they die. Does this answer your question, Gary?"

"Yes, I see that God's mercy must continue with grace to protect us until Jesus comes again."

"Good. Now let's try to define the next word: elect. Will someone read Mark 13:20, please?"

"I can," responded Janet as she quickly found the verse in her New Testament. "If the Lord had not cut short those days, no one would survive. But for the sake of the elect, whom he has chosen, he has shortened them." Looking up, she commented almost immediately, "The elect are God's chosen people, aren't they?"

"Right on, Janet. You got that one. Now let's go to the word 'election,' which needs a Biblical definition."

Before Ted could ask anyone, Carolyn said half aloud, "I think the election represents God's choice of His people."

"Carolyn, I'd say that's correct, but we need some Biblical proof. Do the rest of you understand how Carolyn arrived at this definition?"

"No," several said at once.

Bill's voice seemed to be the loudest, so Ted pointed to him, and Bill asked, "Are the elect chosen by an election?"

"That depends on how you look at it, Bill. This election is not to see if majority of people are going to choose God to be God. This election is about individuals choosing to have faith to believe God. Those who do elect themselves to join God's people, and they are the ones God chooses to be His people. They have been chosen by believing what God says in His word, the Bible. As Hebrews 11:6 says, 'And without faith it is impossible to please God, because anyone who comes to him must believe that he exists and that he rewards those who earnestly seek him.' These are the ones God chooses to be His elect. Each one can choose to believe or not believe. In this election, each person casts a vote for or against their personal faith in God. The Holy Spirit urges them to believe but never coerces. Our individual choosing is how God, from the beginning, has chosen His elect."

"Wow, Ted, I've attended church all my life, but this business of the elect and the election has never been explained to me as simply as this."

"Thanks for your kind remark, Kathy, but you can see that the Bible is quite clear on these meanings when you search them out. Now let's find the Bible meaning of God's purpose."

Tom suddenly interjected. "I've been wondering about that definition."

"Tom, we'll soon find out." Then turning to Carole, Ted asked, "Would you read 1 John 3:8 to us from your King James Bible, please?"

"If you insist," she said with a smile in her voice. "That is if . . . I can find it . . . I know 1 John is located somewhere just a little before Revelation . . . Okay, here it is. 'For this purpose the son of God was manifested, that he might destroy the works of the devil.'"

"That's certainly a straightforward Biblical definition. The purpose of God in sending Jesus was 'to destroy the works of the devil,'" Ted noted. Then he said, "Next, we need to discover the Biblical meaning of the term 'God's call.' For starters, I'll read what Jesus said in Matthew 9:13: 'I have not come to call the righteous, but sinners to repentance.' Since we are all sinners, this means He came to call us all to repent. However, not everybody wants to repent, nor do they. We know that anyone who chooses can reject a call of God.

"The next word that needs a Biblical definition is 'justification.' We learned from Romans 3:23 that all have sinned and, therefore, are wicked and need to be made right with God. So how does mankind get back into favor with God? He can't simply forgive us when we repent. 'The wages of sin is death,' Romans 6:23. But Jesus died in our place, so when we believe in Him, God the Father can forgive us, and we become justified in His sight. In other words, when a wicked person trusts God, this wicked person's faith or belief in Jesus allows God to credit him with a righteousness, which is not his own, and specifically is not given based on any of the man's works. Romans 4:4–5 says, 'Now when a man works, his wages are not credited to him as a gift, but as an obligation. However, to a man who does not work but trusts God who justifies the wicked, his faith is credited as righteousness.' Now look back to Romans 3:24–26. It tells us that we 'are justified freely by his grace through the redemption that came by Christ Jesus.' The last phrase in verse 26 says that God 'justifies the man who has faith in Jesus.' God justifies wicked men simply when they believe in what Jesus has done for them. They repent and are born again and, if possible, will be baptized to publicly demonstrate their belief in Jesus. (Acts 2:38) However, the thief on the cross is an example of someone who came to believe in Jesus and was born again but could not be baptized.

"I've made a list of these words, which includes their Biblical definitions, and at least one proof text," Ted said as he handed a copy of the list to each person.

1. God's mercy—delay in receiving a deserved death, Ephesians 2:4 and Romans 11:32.
2. God's grace—getting the reward of eternal life we don't deserve, Ephesians 2:8–9.
3. God's elect—God's chosen people, Mark13:20.
4. God's election—individuals choosing to have faith to believe God, Hebrews 11:6.
5. God's purpose—Jesus came to destroy the works of the devil, 1 John 3:8.
6. God's call—Jesus came to call sinners to repentance, Matthew 9:13.
7. God's justification—God 'justifies the man who has faith in Jesus,' Romans 3:26.

"Now, with these definitions in mind, we'll be better prepared to understand the texts found in the New Testament, on which Calvin based his doctrine of double predestination, so let us check them out."

"Ted, we thank you for the handout. However, I understand where you're heading," Lee interjected. "But after we've studied the next texts, I'm betting Calvin's teachings will turn out to be right."

"You may be correct, Lee," Ted said, "but for starters, please read aloud to us from two places in the New Testament that Calvin used to substantiate the so-called doctrine of double predestination. They're found in Ephesians 1:3–5 and 11–14 and Romans 8:28–30. Take a few moments to look up the one in Ephesians in your smart phone."

"You want me to read the texts that prove Calvin right?" Lee asked as he fumbled around in the apps. "Oh ah, here it is. Just sit back and listen to how Paul lays out predestination in the first chapter of Ephesians."

"Lay it on us, Lee, but keep an open mind while you read," Ted cautioned. "Be sure to remember the definitions of the words and terms that we just derived from scripture. And please notice that all the pronouns, such as **we, those**, and **you**, are in the plural form. In addition, please check out the context. Paul wrote this epistle to the saints in Ephesus, who had been predestined as a group and not as an individual saint."

With those instructions, the others listened intently as Lee began reading.

> Praise be to the God and Father of our Lord Jesus Christ, who blessed **us** in the heavenly realms with every spiritual blessing in Christ. For he chose **us** in him before the creation of the world to be holy and blameless in his sight. In love, he predestined **us** to be adopted as his **sons** through Jesus Christ in accordance with his pleasure and will.

"And as you suggested, Ted, I'll drop down to verse 11."

> In him **we** were **chosen**, having been predestined according to the plan of him who works out everything in conformity with the **purpose** of his will, in order that **we** who were first to hope in Christ, might be for the praise of his glory. And **you** also were included in Christ when **you** heard the word of truth, the gospel of **your** salvation. Having believed, **you** were marked in him with a seal, the promised Holy Spirit, who is a deposit guaranteeing **our** inheritance until the redemption of **those** who are God's possession—to the praise of his glory?

"Wow, Ted," Pauline noted, "I see what you mean. All the pronouns are in the plural form, and the word 'sons' is also plural. This information tells us that a group of people, not an individual person, is whom God had predestined."

As Lee looked up from his smart phone, Ted asked him, "Did you notice the words **chosen** and **purpose** as you read verse 11?"

"No, Ted, I read so fast I must have overlooked them."

"Well, look back at verse 11 again, and you will see both words are there. Recall from the definitions that the **chosen** people are His **elect** and the **purpose** of God is to destroy the works of the devil."

"Okay, Ted, I'll read verses 11 and 12 again: 'In him **we** were **chosen**, having been predestined according to the plan of him who works out everything in conformity with the **purpose** of his will, in order that **we** who were first to hope in Christ, might be for the praise of his glory.'

"See, Ted, Calvin is right!" Lee almost yelled. "These folks were 'predestined according to the plan,' God's plan."

"But, Lee, and the rest of you, notice what verse 13 says. They 'were included in Christ when **you** heard the word of truth, the gospel of your salvation. Having believed, **you** were marked in him with a seal.' They were not included in Christ until after they heard and believed the gospel. Then the Holy Spirit could mark and seal them to become part of the group who were predestined from the beginning. Now, Lee, please read verses 7 and 8, which I had you skip."

"Okay, Ted. 'In him **we** have redemption through his blood, the forgiveness of sins, in accordance with the riches of God's **grace** that he lavished on us with all wisdom and understanding. And he made known to **us** the ministry of his will according to his good pleasure, which he **purposed** in Christ, to put into effect when the times will have reached their fulfillment—to bring all things in heaven and on earth together under one head, even Christ.'"

"Did you notice, Lee, that God's purpose in Christ did not occur until 'the times will have reached their fulfillment'?"

Howard, who had remained quiet up until then, unexpectedly declared, "This tells us that God had predestined Christ to destroy the works of the devil in us by lavishing us with His grace."

"And this happened at the time of its fulfillment through 'the mystery of His will according to His good pleasure, which He purposed in Christ,'" Hank reiterated from the text.

Ted practically shouted, "I love it when the Holy Spirit helps us catch on to what is being read from God's word." Then pausing for a few seconds, he asked, "Lee, would you please continue reading, but this time from Romans 8:28–30?"

With some reluctance and a slight delay while he looked for the text in his smart phone, he began.

> And **we** know that in all things God works for the good of **those** who **love him**, who have been **called** according to his **purpose**. For **those** God foreknew he also predestined to be conformed to the likeness of his Son, that he might be the firstborn among **many brothers**. And **those** he predestined, he also **called**; **those** he **called**, he also justified; **those** he justified, he also glorified.

"I see," Kathy broke in. "All the pronouns in both Ephesians and Romans are in the plural form. Therefore, it is clear to me that God applies predestination to groups of people. And the term 'many brothers' also refers to a group, but He calls only those who love Him according to His **purpose**, which is to destroy the work of the devil. Each person has to decide to accept or reject God's call and choose whether or not to join God's chosen people by believing in Jesus."

Observing that others were beginning to understand these New Testament passages, Ted said, with a gleeful note in his voice, "I'm overjoyed to see you catching on so quickly. In addition to these texts, however, the observation that a group of people is being identified as predestined and not an individual applies to four other texts not yet mentioned. They are John 15:15, where Jesus is addressing **friends.** In John 17:24, Jesus uses the plural pronoun **those**. In Romans 11:2, Paul addresses **people**. And Peter spoke to **strangers** in 1 Peter 1:1–2.

"Acts 2:22–23 and another place in 1 Peter 1:20 also tell us that God had chosen Jesus before the creation to be the sacrificial Lamb of God. The sacrifice of Jesus would be needed only if evil arose after He created intelligent beings who could make freewill choices. Therefore, God could foreknow what Jesus would do if evil arose. All the other texts refer to a group of people God has chosen. He can predestine only people who have accepted His grace and, through faith, believe in Jesus."

Ted continued. "God could foresee before creating mankind that if He gave them the ability to make freewill choices, some or all might choose selfishness. If that should occur, He had, in advance, made a plan that could redeem some or all those who chose evil by having Christ die a sacrificial death in their place. God could be both just and forgiving to sinners (Romans 3:21–26) if they made a freewill choice to believe in Jesus. When this information regarding predestination in all these 'texts' is applied in its plural form, a congregation of people becomes evident—a group of believers God could foreknow would exist in each generation. Collectively, this group He could predestine to be saved, but if humans have free will, God could not foreknow who would choose to join the group. However, when anyone allows the Holy Spirit to persuade them to make Jesus Lord of their lives and to repent of selfishness, they become God's elect and form part of His chosen people, known as the election."

Lee, noting that his Calvinistic understanding of predestination had started to erode, asked, "Are there any texts to show that God doesn't know what humans are going to choose?"

"Yes," replied Ted. "The first one mentioned in the Bible involves the *Akadah*, the story of Abraham receiving divine instruction to offer his son, Isaac, as a human sacrifice to God. This story is found in Genesis 22. The first verse says, 'God tested Abraham.' We all know how the story ends. Just when Abraham raises the knife to slay Isaac, who was bound on the altar, the angel yells for him to stop. A ram caught in a nearby thicket is substituted for Isaac. Both father and son went home happy. Verse 12 states, 'Now I know that you fear God,' meaning that, before the test, God did not know how Abraham would choose.

"The second example is found in Daniel 10:12–14. It tells us that Gabriel tried unsuccessfully for twenty-one days to get the prince of Persia to change his mind, so Michael came to help. This use of persistent urging shows that God never forces a decision on someone, and neither does He know the outcome ahead of time.

"The last example comes from Apostle Peter's second letter, chapter 3, verse 9. Speaking of God, Peter says, 'He is patient with you, not wanting anyone to perish, but everyone to come to repentance.' Last week, we learned in Episode II if God had foreknown what each of our choices would be, or as in the first part of Episode III, He had decreed before the creation, every choice we were going make, then God would not be wishing for all to come to repentance. Because He would, either by His foreknowledge or divine decree, already have known where everyone's eternal address was going to be. The notion of individual predestination contradicts the 'whosoever believes' of John 3:16 (KJV) and the 'whosoever will' of Revelation 22:17 (KJV). Each indicates that we can make independent, uncoerced, freewill choices.

"Individual predestination relegates God's mercy and grace into meaningless paradigms. Why would God extend mercy to someone He previously had created for destruction or one He had already created for salvation? The same idea applies to God's grace. How could His grace save someone He had already predestined to hell or be responsible for saving someone He had created to be saved? In either case, God would be responsible for each person's eternal destiny. From these scenarios, we can see that human free will must exist. Otherwise, how could God obtain requited love from someone He had preprogrammed to love Him or from a person whom He knew would choose to love Him before he was created? Also, if divine fiat insured our place in heaven, why would Peter extol his readers in 2 Peter 1:10 to make their 'calling and election sure' if both were already guaranteed?"

"I still think," Lee interrupted, "that Calvin was correct when he applied these predestination statements to individuals instead of groups. I maintain this position because I've read ahead into Romans 9, where Paul is talking about individuals."

"With respect to predestination, Lee, I had trouble understanding that chapter as well," Ted said. "However, to ferret out the meaning of what Paul is telling his readers in Romans 9, we must keep in mind the definitions we elicited from scripture."

"But delving into this chapter," Janice interrupted, "will have to wait till the next time we meet because it is already late."

With that being said, she dismissed the group.

All Biblical quotes in this chapter are from the NIV version of the Bible unless otherwise noted in the places used.

Summary of Man's Free Will and God's Sovereignty (Part Two)

1. God's mercy—a delay in receiving the inevitable result of sin, namely death, Ephesians 2:4 and Romans 11:32.
2. God's grace—getting a reward we don't deserve, Ephesians 2:8–9.
3. God's elect—God's chosen people, Mark 13:20.

4. God's election—individuals choosing to have faith to believe God, Hebrews 11:6.

5. God's purpose—Jesus came to destroy the works of the devil, 1 John 3:8.

6. God's call—Jesus came to call sinners to repentance, Matthew 9:13.

7. God's justification—God 'justifies the man who has faith in Jesus,' Romans 3:26.

8. In Ephesians 1:3–5 and 11–14 and Romans 8:28–30, all pronouns are plural. They refer to groups of people that compose God's church or His people down through the ages.

9. Those who believe in Jesus and accept His sacrifice for their sins elect themselves to join God's church and become part of His election. In every generation, this has been true. Before Jesus came, God's elect believed that God would send a redeemer, and after Jesus came, the elect believe in Him.

10. Several Biblical references were given, which show that God didn't know if a given person would accept or reject His plan of redemption until after they chose. God knows everything except the next choice anyone is going to make.

11. Every person is free to accept or reject the sacrifice of Jesus for their salvation. No one is forced either way.

Chapter Three

Man's Free Will and Romans 9

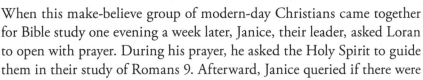

When this make-believe group of modern-day Christians came together for Bible study one evening a week later, Janice, their leader, asked Loran to open with prayer. During his prayer, he asked the Holy Spirit to guide them in their study of Romans 9. Afterward, Janice queried if there were any unresolved issues or questions left over from their last meeting.

Carolyn raised her hand and, after being recognized, said, "Last time, our study concluded near the end of verse 30 in Romans 8. During this past week, I've read the last few remaining verses of that chapter and would like to understand how they fit with Calvin's predestination. He applied predestination to individuals only, but we learned it should be applied only to groups."

"Good," several others echoed Carolyn, implying that they too had questions about these verses.

So Janice turned to Ted and Lee, who were sitting across each other, and asked, "Because our study for the last couple of sessions has turned into a debate between you two about the doctrine of predestination, would either of you be willing to answer Carolyn's question?"

"I'll give it my best shot," Lee replied.

Janice quickly turned to Carolyn and told her to fire away.

"Well, to me, verses 31–39 tell us that 'if God is for **us,** who can be against **us?**' Therefore, nothing should be able to separate God's love from **those** he has **chosen.**"

Then looking at Lee, Carolyn stated, "Here again, as Ted pointed out last week, Paul used the plural pronouns **us** and **those,** which were restricted to God's **chosen.** So with respect to God's love, what difference would there be if the Almighty predestined a single individual or a group to be loved by the Deity and—"

Lee interrupted her in mid-sentence. "I don't think it would make any difference."

"But, Lee," Carolyn continued, "I also want to know the criteria God uses to choose those He is going to love."

Before Lee could respond to Carolyn's second question, Ted broke in with "Lee, I think you should hold your answers to both of Carolyn's questions until we review Calvin's position regarding predestination. So on your smart phone, would you bring up the quote from him that you read at our first gathering?"

"Sure, Ted, give me a sec while I find it . . . Okay, here it is. Let me read it again."

> We call predestination God's eternal counsel by which he has determined what he wishes to do with each and every person. For He does not create them all in like condition, but appoints some to eternal life and others to eternal damnation. Thus, according to the end for which a person has been created, we say that he is predestined to death or to life.
>
> —John Calvin's *Institutes of the Christian Religion*, p. 467

"With this concise statement of Calvin clearly in mind, Lee, please be careful in answering Carolyn's questions," Ted cautioned, then continued. "As I understand it, Calvin's doctrine of predestination means that God predestined each person before their creation, either to eternal life or to eternal damnation. Is my understanding correct?"

"Yes, Ted," Lee answered.

"Then in your opinion," Ted continued, "do you believe Calvin's compact statement indicates that God's love for a given individual is displayed when He predestines that person with eternal life?"

"Yes," Lee quickly replied.

"Well, Lee, if that's the case, then God should have predestined everyone to enjoy eternal life with Him forever because He loves everybody. Therefore, your 'yes' answer has to be wrong."

"Ted, from what scripture did you derive this precept that God loves everyone?"

"John 3:16, 'For God so loved the world that he gave his one and only son, that whoever believes in him shall not perish but have eternal life.'"

"Lee, this verse teaches that only believers get eternal life. But because God loves everybody, it also answers Carolyn's first question regarding why God loves a person or a group. In addition, it shows that God doesn't use His all-inclusive love as a criterion to predestine those who get eternal life and those who don't. So in reverse, I'll ask you this: Is a person's love for God dependent upon God first predestining that person to love Him?"

"Yes, Ted, 1 John 4:19 says, '**We** love because he first loved **us**.'"

"Okay, Lee, I like your use of scripture, but did you notice the plural pronouns **we** and **us**?"

"No, Ted." Then Lee asked, "What difference would plural pronouns make? Jesus' parable of the lost sheep indicates that God cares for an individual person as well as a group."

"You're right, Lee, but why would God, represented in this parable by the shepherd, need to go out looking for a lost sheep if that sheep already had been predestined with eternal life?"

"I'm not sure, Ted, but this parable shows that God cares for individuals as well as groups."

"I'll give you that, Lee. But let's try to answer Carolyn's second question."

"Okay," Lee agreed, thinking to himself that Ted had given him a break by not pressing the issue further as to why God rescued a lost sheep already predestined with eternal life.

"So, Lee, would it be impossible for an individual to hate God if he or she had been predestined to love Him?"

"Yes, I believe it would, Ted, because once God predestines someone either to eternal life or damnation, that person can't change his attitude toward God."

"So, if I understand Calvin's statement correctly, Lee, is every individual's love or hate for God dependent upon which way God predestines each one before He created them—yes or no?"

"Yes."

"Great Scott!" Tom exclaimed. Then looking directly at Lee, he asked, "Does this doctrine of predestination that Calvin taught teach that God has to predestine an individual one way or the other before that person can love or hate Him back?"

"Yes, Tom," Lee responded. "And I'm quite sure these concepts will become clearer as we get into our study of Romans 9." Then Lee paused for a moment, realizing that neither he nor Ted had answered Carolyn's second question.

Janice, noting Lee's hesitation, inquired of Carolyn if her questions had been answered.

"The first one, yes. I liked Lee's reference to the lost sheep parable. It tells us that God loves individuals, as well as groups, and so does John 3:16. But if Calvin's brand of predestination is true, Lee has not given us any Biblical criteria that God uses to decide which way a person is going to be predestined before God creates a given individual."

"We just have to leave that up to the all-knowing God!" Lee interjected.

"Lee," Ted queried, "what do you mean by the term 'all-knowing God'?"

"God's foreknowledge, Ted. I like Calvin's definition of it, which I have in my smart phone."

"Good grief, Lee, do you have a complete copy of Calvin's *Institutes of the Christian Religion* in your phone?" asked Garry.

"No, Garry, but after the discussion that we had during our first get-together, I researched a copy of Calvin's book at our church library and found references on the topics of foreknowledge, predestination, and how God chooses which way a person is going to be created. These references I found on pages 466 and 467, which I copied into my phone."

"So, Lee, what does Calvin have to say about God's foreknowledge?"

"I'll show you, Ted, with another quote from him.

> When we attribute foreknowledge to God, we mean that everything has always been, and forever remains, in his full view, so that in terms of his knowledge there is nothing which is either future or past. Instead, all things are present to him—so present indeed that he does not see them, as it were, as mental images, as we do who need imagination to make more or less visible the things preserved in our memory. God observes and beholds them just as they are, as if they were actually before him.

We affirm that this foreknowledge covers the whole wide world and with it every creature.

—Calvin, pp. 466–467

"However, Calvin has something to say about this on the same page where the former quote is found. I have a copy of it right here in my smart phone. Give me a sec, and I'll pull it up. Here it is . . ."

We say that those whom he calls to salvation he receives in his free mercy, without regard to their personal worth. On the other hand, we say that entry into life is denied those whom he wishes to abandon to perdition, and that comes about through his secret and incomprehensible, but just and equitable, judgment.

—Calvin, p. 467

"Wow, Lee!" Ted exclaimed. "Calvin says the criteria God uses to foreordain which way He plans to create people 'comes about through his secret and incomprehensible, but just and equitable, judgment.' Calvin, p. 467. How can we know His decision is just if His method of choosing is secret?"

For her benefit, Ted predicted that Carolyn's second question would be answered, if scripture proved Calvin's predestination doctrine false. To start in this direction, he cited Jeremiah 26:2–3. "Tell them everything I commanded you; do not omit a word. Perhaps they will listen and each will turn from his evil way. Then I will relent and not bring on them the disaster I was planning because of the evil they had done." But before going there, Ted posed another question to Lee, taken from Jeremiah 26:3: "God told Jeremiah to tell the people to turn from their evil ways. But how could they, if God already had fixed their eternal destinies by divine fiat before creation?"

Lee, realizing his dilemma, just sat thinking.

Bill took advantage of this break in the discussion and spoke up with his deep voice. He asked, "Regardless of the implications brought forth to the contrary, I still can't help but wonder why two New Testament writers used the term 'predestination' in the first place, that is, if they didn't really mean it the way it seems to indicate?"

"Thank you, Bill, that's what I was wondering," Kathy quickly inserted. This was followed by similar comments from Hank and Howard.

Seeing that Bill's question had momentarily diverted the group's thinking away from his quandary and that others in the group were having doubts about Ted's anti-Calvin predestination rhetoric, Lee gleefully responded with "That's what I've been trying to get you folks to understand all along."

"Listen up, everyone," Ted quickly shot back. "Understanding what the New Testament writers meant when they used the word 'predestination' is only one of several problems we will encounter in Romans 9. However, the most pressing will be to learn, if scripture rejects Calvin's predestination doctrine, and with it, the need to answer Carolyn's second question regarding the criteria God uses to predestine some to eternal life or some to damnation. So when Paul said in Romans 8 that it was impossible for anything to separate God's chosen people (plural) from God's love, this also would apply to individuals that God chose mentioned in chapter 9."

Lee, with a triumphant sounding voice, jumped in. "Ted, this is exactly why I believe the New Testament teaches that God predestines individuals and not just groups of believers as you claimed when we got together last week."

"Thanks, Lee, you may be correct, so let's begin by reading the first four verses of Romans 9. Barbara, would you do the honors, please?"

"Yes, I'd be delighted." Opening her New Testament to the verses, she read, "I speak the truth in Christ—I am not lying, my conscience confirms it in the Holy Spirit—I have great sorrow and unceasing anguish in my heart. For I could wish that I myself were cursed and cut off from Christ for the sake of my **brothers**, **those** of my own race, the **people** of Israel. **Theirs** is the adoption as **sons**; **theirs** the divine glory, the covenants, the revealing of the law, the temple worship and the promises."

When she looked up, Ted took over. "Let's assume that Paul's understanding of predestination was the same as Calvin's, namely that God had, before the creation, capriciously predestined each person either to eternal life or damnation. If that had been the case, Paul would have thought that all his unbelieving brothers were stuck where God had assigned them. If he believed this to be the case, Lee, do you think he would have started chapter 9 by wishing himself cursed and cutoff from Christ in order to figuratively save his kinsmen, a group of God's chosen people, the Jews?"

"Yes," Lee replied, "He probably would as Paul only wished that there was a way to bring salvation to his Jewish brothers, even though he knew they already had been predestined to death."

"If that's the case, Lee, how do you explain Romans 11:14? Here Paul says, 'I may somehow arouse my own people to envy and save some of them.' If the apostle understood his use of 'predestination' to mean what Calvin thought it meant, then how could he turn around and say that some of Israel would be saved?"

"He wouldn't!" exclaimed Annie.

"And, Bill," Ted interjected, "if Paul's belief about predestination was the same as Calvin's, do you think he would contradict himself in the text I showed you in Romans 11:32?"

"No, Ted, he probably wouldn't."

"But what about you, Lee?" Ted asked.

"I don't know. All I know is that Paul names six individuals, right after what Barbara read, whose eternal destinies seem to have been foretold by God's foreknowledge. This list of individual names might go a long way toward finding an answer to Carolyn's second question."

"I think we need to read verse 5 of chapter 9 before we start over the names listed. So, Barbara, would you read it for us?" Ted asked.

"Sure, Ted. 'Theirs are the patriarchs, and from them is traced the human ancestry of Christ, who is God over all, forever praised! Amen.'"

"Notice, Lee, that Paul follows verse 5 by giving examples, which show how God traced the human ancestry of Jesus through them. Would you agree?" Ted questioned.

"Sure. The first one mentioned is Abraham."

"Yes, Lee, that's obvious. But think, did you get to choose your ancestors before you were born?"

"No."

"That's right, but Jesus could, and He did. The first patriarch He chose was Abraham followed by his promised second son (Isaac). In turn, God chose Jacob, the second of the twins born to Isaac and Rebecca, instead of Esau, the firstborn. This latter choice occurred while both were still in the womb and happened before they 'had done anything good or bad.'"

"See, that's what I've been trying to tell you, Ted, God chose Jacob before he was even born."

"Yes, Lee, but for what was he chosen? Was it to be one of Jesus' progenitors from the seed of Abraham or to be predestined for salvation?" Ted asked.

"I believe the latter, Ted. Just listen as I read the last part of the sentence, starting with 'in order that God's purpose in election might stand: not by works but by him who calls—she was told. The older will serve the younger.' See, that's what I've been saying exactly. God, in this case, predestined both Jacob and Esau before they were born, one for life and one for damnation."

"I have trouble with your last statement, Lee," Ted noted, "because, if God had predestined Jacob and the others, without their consent, for life or death before their creation, why would He need to call them, if their eternal destiny had been determined already?"

"But, Ted, who said anything about being called?"

"Lee, you just read the words 'by him who calls.'"

Most of the group laughed a little at Lee, who seemed to be getting a little frustrated.

"But, Ted," Lee continued, "let me read what Paul says next. 'Just as it was written: Jacob I loved, but Esau I hated.' Verses 10–13 tell us that in order for God's purpose in the election to stand, He chose Jacob for salvation and Esau for damnation." Now Lee thought to himself, *Let's see how Ted gets around this.*

"Lee, the words 'Jacob I loved, but Esau I hated' were not said to Rebecca but instead were uttered by the prophet Malachi about a thousand years later, which referred to the nations that came from these two individuals. Also, Lee, you didn't answer my question. If, according to Calvin, each one had been predestined for life or death before their creation, why would God need to call them?"

"I don't know."

"Well, Lee, please remember the definitions that we derived last week from the Bible. God's purpose in election was to destroy the works of the devil, and that's why God the Father sent Jesus, who came to earth to redeem anyone who chooses to believe in Him and repent. The verse 11 of Romans 9 may hint at part of an answer to Carolyn's second question, in that God does not choose people based on their past behaviors. Therefore, if God had predestined each person before He created them, then there would have been no behavior on which He could have made a choice. The fact that Apostle Paul never mentions anything about the behaviors of the twins indicates that he didn't believe in singular predestination. Otherwise, he would have known that their behaviors had been decreed by divine fiat.

"So, Lee, even though these early patriarchs didn't know everything for which they were being called, they accepted it by faith and contributed a small amount of their genetic material to the human side of Christ. Though a miniscule contribution, through Christ, it eventually became a blessing to all nations of the world.

"The election is simply God's choice of people who have accepted God's call and by faith have come to believe. In the womb, neither Jacob nor Esau could have chosen. However, because of each patriarch's faith, God, in succession, chose Abraham, Sarah, Isaac, Rebecca, and Jacob to be among the first of many the Almighty chose to become progenitors of Jesus. What criteria God used to make those decisions we are not told, except that it was not based on the later behaviors of Esau or Jacob. Likewise, God did not choose Rahab the harlot or Ruth the Moabite to become part of the human heritage of Jesus based upon their respective behaviors. From these examples, we learn that God didn't use human behavior as criteria for choosing people that He supposedly will predestine one way or the other. They voluntarily chose to join the ever-increasing group, God's invisible church, which was predestined to be redeemed from eternal ruin by Jesus.

"We mortals are never able to know all the reasons why God chooses certain people to do heaven's work. Sometimes God uses those who are not even among the elect to do something extra special. King Nebuchadnezzar and later King Darius are two Biblical examples. In more recent times, He used King James I of England to finance the translation of the Bible into English from the original Hebrew and Greek languages. However, did you know that King James was a homosexual with more than one male lover? Maybe he was bisexual as he did marry and father an heir to his throne. Regardless, however, for more than four hundred years, that translation of the Bible into English had been known as the King James Version. It has borne his name, that of a gay man."

"You're kidding." Lee almost gulped, which was echoed by several others.

"No, I'm not. Look it up in Google," Ted suggested. "Now back to Romans 9."

"Yeah, Ted, let's go there," Lee urged, "but know this—I'm still not convinced that Calvin's teaching is wrong."

"That's okay, Lee. So to help us get back on track, would you read out loud verses 14–18 of Romans 9?"

After a short pause, while bringing up these verses on his smart phone, Lee began. "What then shall we say? Is God unjust? Not at all! For He says to Moses, 'I will have mercy on whom I have mercy, and I will have compassion on whom I have compassion. It does not, therefore, depend on man's desire or effort, but on God's mercy. For the Scripture says to Pharaoh: I raised you up for this very purpose, that I might display my power in you and that my name might be proclaimed in all the earth. Therefore, God has mercy on whom he wants to have mercy, and he hardens whom he wants to harden.'"

"Ted," Pat spoke up unexpectedly, "it's difficult for me to understand this passage outside of Calvin's understanding of predestination. These verses seem to say that God showers mercy on whomever He pleases and hardens whomever He pleases."

Lee, laughingly clapped his hands a couple of times, realizing that another person in their group was leaning toward Calvin and his understanding of predestination. His glee was abated a little, however, when Gayle raised her hand for Janice to recognize.

After receiving an affirmative nod, she said, "Please excuse me, Ted, but I need to review the first two of those definitions we derived last week from the Bible in order to keep them in mind as we proceed."

"And so do I," chided Kathy.

"Gayle, do you mean mercy and grace?" Ted questioned.

"Yes, but especially on whom they are bestowed and how long they last."

"Remember, Gayle, Hans defined God's mercy as postponement of receiving an inevitable undesirable result, namely, death, and Dave pointed out that God's grace was the opposite of mercy. It meant obtaining an undeserved reward. Do you remember that, Gayle?"

"Yes, I recall both of those definitions, but the text that Lee just read seems to indicate that God showers mercy capriciously on some folks and withholds it from others. It seems Paul is saying that God unfairly predestines some to be hardened so they cannot receive His mercy."

"Gayle, a casual reading of these verses does seem to indicate your perception to be right, but don't forget, mercy is not God dispensing a blessing on someone but rather is withholding a kind of inevitable punishment for a time. Therefore, because 'the wages of sin is death' and 'all have sinned,' if anyone is alive, that alone indicates that God, through His mercy, has temporarily postponed the inevitable result of eternal death on that person."

"Ted, does the Bible say that everyone receives mercy?"

"Yes, Gayle, don't you remember Romans 11:32, the verse that we studied last week?"

"Somewhat, but please read it to us again."

"Okay, Gayle, I have it right here," Ted said. "For God has bound all men over to disobedience so that he may have mercy on them all."

"So, Ted, does this mean that anybody who's alive is experiencing God's mercy?"

"Yes, Gayle. If God did not withhold the inevitable undesired result of sin, everyone who has sinned would be dead already, leaving no one on whom He could dispense His grace because we've all sinned."

"Ted, this means that God's mercy always has to precede His grace, doesn't it?"

"You got that right, Gayle."

"But, Ted," Pat interrupted again, "how long does God's mercy last and when is it withdrawn from an individual? 'Is God unjust,' as Paul asks in Romans 9:14?"

"Those are two great questions, Pat. So for an answer to your first question, let's have Lee read Paul's recitation of Exodus 33:19, which Paul quotes in Romans 9:15. Will you read verse 15 to us, Lee?"

"Sure, Ted, beginning with the quote, 'I will have mercy on whom I have mercy, and I will have compassion on whom I have compassion.' And verse 16 says, 'It does not depend on Man's desire or effort.'"

"But, Ted, this verse doesn't answer Pat's question as to how long God grants mercy to an individual."

"I agree, Lee, however, would you read the first word of Romans 9:16 from the New International Version (NIV) to us again?"

"Okay . . . It's the word 'it,' Ted, but for what does the pronoun 'it' stand?"

Before Ted could answer, Pat announced, "The word 'it' stands for God's compassion."

Then Ted said, "When I looked up this word in the dictionary, 'compassion' is defined as having 'sorrow for the sufferings or troubles of another or others, accompanied with an urge to help.'"

"That sounds a little like grace just starting to take effect," Pat noted. "And the text says it doesn't depend on any 'man's desire or effort.' Nobody can earn God's compassion, can they?"

"That's right, Pat. Even though verse 16 doesn't answer your question completely, it does prepare us to discover in verses 17 and 18 how long God withheld a punishment on the pharaoh and what caused God to stop. If we study the experience of the pharaoh in Exodus and determine when God withdrew mercy on that individual, this story also will help us see when God withdraws mercy from anyone else and understand why this action can be just."

Having forced herself to remain silent during this session, Karen couldn't hold back any longer. Breaking in, she said, "Well, Ted, that may be easy for you to say, but I've had a theological hang up about this part of Romans 9 ever since I was a kid back in Sunday school. I had forgotten all about it until reminded just now. It has to do with God hardening the pharaoh's heart so God could punish him later for not doing what God had told him to do. This doesn't seem fair. So, Ted, could you explain this to me?"

"Karen, thank you for pointing out something that had slipped my mind to mention. Verse 18 says that God hardens anyone He wants to harden."

Lee, muttering under his breath, said, "I'm going to love Ted's feeble attempt at explaining this to Karen because it seems she has painted him into a corner."

"Karen," Ted began, "with respect to hardening, some folks believe this isolated statement, which says that God hardens whomever He wants to harden, is an example of how God hardens a person to not do something good so that He can punish that person later for not doing the thing He had hardened him not to do.

"Actually, God's hardening of the pharaoh's heart, to which Apostle Paul refers in verse 18, seems to make it impossible for the pharaoh to obey God and allow the Israelites to leave Egypt. With a quick read of this account in Exodus, it seems like God acted unfairly toward the pharaoh by encouraging him to disobey and then punishing him for disobeying."

"Yeah, that's why I've had a hang up about what this verse means," Karen said quietly.

"Well, Karen, and the rest of you, a careful evaluation of the Exodus story shows that God did not actually harden the pharaoh's heart until He struck Egypt with the sixth plague. God allowed the pharaoh at least five chances to stop hardening his own heart and comply with the Almighty's demands before He hardened the pharaoh's heart even more.

"The pharaoh, being the most powerful man on Earth at the time, was not going to submit to the demands of any god and especially the God of his slaves. If he submitted to the demands of the God of heaven, this would mean that he and his gods were weaker than the Hebrew God. Therefore, his own selfish pride forbade him to obey.

"God, in scripture, said to the pharaoh, 'I raised you up for this very purpose; that I might display my power in you and that my name might be proclaimed in all the earth.' God had raised up the pharaoh to be the most powerful man on Earth at that time. If, at first, against his own stubborn tendency, the pharaoh had given in to God's demands, this of itself would have magnified God's name. But after the pharaoh's own stubbornness was augmented even more when God hardened his heart, starting with the sixth plague, his increased refusal to obey only magnified God's name and power to a greater degree, until the pharaoh was forced to comply after the tenth plague. Under these circumstances, God was not unfair with the pharaoh by hardening his heart.

"Now we can answer Pat's two questions," Ted continued. "God allows His mercy to last until He sees that a given person is not going to stop rebelling against Him. Then, when His mercy is withdrawn, God will not be unjust even if He hardens that person some more."

"Wow, Ted, now I can understand why God wasn't unfair in His dealings with old pharaoh."

With that assertion of Karen, everyone, including Lee, remained quiet for a few moments as they thought it over.

Then Gary broke in. "I'm sorry, Ted, but when I read verses 19–24 of Romans 9, I have a tough time divorcing my thinking from the predestination teaching of Calvin."

Seeing that at least one person besides himself in the group was still leaning toward Calvinism, Lee shouted, "Right on!"

Ted, ignoring Lee's outburst, said, "Well, Gary, will you read those verses to us beginning with verse 19?"

"Sure, Ted, give me a second while I find them . . . 'One of you will say—'"

"Excuse me, Gary," Ted interrupted, "I forgot to remind you that Paul, in this passage, asks a series of questions. Some of them are long and convoluted. So try to count the number of questions as you read."

"Okay, Ted."

"Good, Gary." Ted cautioned, "But this time count the number of questions as you read."

"Okay, Ted."

"One of you will say to me: Then why does God still blame us? For who resists his will? But who are you, O man, to talk back to God? Shall what is formed say to Him who formed it, why did you make me like this? Does not the potter have the right to make out of the same lump of clay some pottery for noble purposes and some for common use? What if God, choosing to show his wrath and make His power known, bore with great patience the objects of his wrath—prepared for destruction? What if he did this to make the riches of His glory known to the objects of his mercy, whom he prepared for glory—even us whom he also called, not only from the Jews, but also from the Gentiles?"

When Gary finished, Ted inquired of the group, "How many questions did you count?"

There was a relatively short pause as everyone recounted. Some said six and some seven.

"I counted seven question marks in my NIV Bible," Loran noted.

"And I counted six in my King James Version (KJV)!" Carole exclaimed.

"You're both right," Ted said. "The translators of the NIV divided the last question into two because it was so long. In the KJV, how many English words are needed to make that question?"

Carole, after quickly counting, said, "In my KJV, there are sixty-four."

"Imagine what that would be like in Greek," Linda punted.

"It's all Greek to me anyway," Gayle muttered rather loudly.

After the snickering stopped, Ted commented, "Paul wrote some of these questions in long sentences. So when they were translated into English from Greek, it should come as no surprise that they contain many words as well. This portion of Paul's writing, however, is not as difficult to understand as it might seem. First, let's write out each question, and then, as far as possible, we'll try to answer each one from scripture. So will someone read the first one to us again?"

"Then why does God blame us?" Barbara read quickly.

"Okay, write it down in your notebook," Ted suggested and then continued. "Paul, undoubtedly prompted from the pharaoh's experience, seems to be asking, 'How can God hold **us** accountable for not doing something He told **us** to do and then harden **us** so we can't?'"

Lee quickly jumped in. "Yeah, Ted, that's exactly why Calvin has to be right. God predestines some people to damnation and these folks He hardens, making it impossible for them to obey."

"Lee, if God, according to a Calvin mind-set, had already predestined the pharaoh to hell by a divine decree, why would He offer mercy to the pharaoh at least five times before hardening him? Each of the first five plagues actually postponed the pharaoh's earthly punishment and gave him a reason to comply and avoid the final consequence later in the Red Sea. In the question at hand, however, Paul included himself and everyone else in it when he used the plural pronoun **us**. This question indicated that Paul knew that God holds all of **us** responsible for our individual choices, with regard to our rebelling against Him. Otherwise, if each one's eternal outcome had already been decided by God's decree, He couldn't hold **us** responsible.

"Think about this: Paul himself had experienced God's mercy on the road to Damascus when Jesus struck him blind for persecuting His church. Unlike the pharaoh, Paul ceased to resist God's will after receiving only one 'prompting.' Instead of eternal death, Paul received his sight back and God's grace as well. However, if in stubborn selfish pride, we refuse to obey, God can and does bring trials to us now with which He endeavors to persuade us to change our minds, maybe even more than five times. Reluctantly, He will withdraw His mercy, but in the end, if we persist in stubbornness, He ceases to withhold our deserved punishment and, thereby, make the stubborn choice ours. On these folks, God can't dispense His grace because they don't want it.

"I hope this answers Paul's first question adequately. Does anyone of you have anything to add?" A long pause followed. But because no one spoke up, Ted asked, "Will someone read the next question?"

"I can," Carolyn volunteered, "and it is 'Who resists His will?'"

Ted waited for a moment while everyone wrote it down and then began. "From what we've learned already, anyone who is alive can reject

God's command until, like the pharaoh, God sees that a given person's mind is fixed. Reluctantly, He finally gives up and withdraws His mercy. Hardening on that person's heart may then begin, which prepares the way for receiving the result of eternal death, either then or later." Then Ted asked, "So does anyone have a comment or question before we proceed?"

Pauline raised her hand and after receiving Ted's nod, inquired, "Why in the world would Paul fire seven questions in a row at us without giving any answers?"

"Yeah, that's what I was wondering," Dave chimed in.

"Well, I was hoping that someone would bring this up," Ted responded. "So thank you, Pauline and Dave, for you collectively questioning Apostle Paul's teaching methods. First of all, he was the most educated of all the apostles, having been tutored by Gamaliel in Jerusalem. He spoke and wrote both Hebrew and Greek fluently, the latter being the main language spoken in Rome. Hoping to travel there soon, he endeavored to introduce himself, via this letter, to the Roman Christians living in the capital of the empire before his arrival. They undoubtedly were more sophisticated than the folks living in the outback of Asia Minor, where he had previously preached the gospel. Therefore, in this epistle written in Greek, he used a more profound approach to explain the basics of Christianity. Having learned from a rabbi, he followed a common method of rabbinical teaching, by answering a question with a question. Therefore, care is needed to ferret out the answer to each question as we proceed."

"Wow," Tom noted. "This guy was smart. No wonder we can't sail through this ancient letter like learning to read Dick and Jane back in the first grade."

"Tom, what are you talking about, and who are Dick and Jane?" asked Karen, the youngest of the group.

The older members all began to laugh, so Mabel explained to Karen that many years ago Dick and Jane were imaginary characters in vogue at the time to first-grade readers.

"Oh."

Then endeavoring to redirect the discussion back to Romans, Ted asked Pauline if his explanation had helped her understand why Paul taught with repetitive, rhetorical questions.

"Yes, but because Paul tries to answer one question with another, and another, and another, etc., why don't we have Lee read in succession all the remaining questions while we write them in our notes before we tackle the third," Pauline suggested.

"Good idea," several agreed.

"So, Lee, would you read all the questions over again from your smart phone? Please pause after each one so that all of us, including you, can write them down in our notes. Anyway, we've already written down the first two."

"Sure, Ted, hold on while I find the place again." Then reading and pausing, he proceeded.

1. "Then why does God still blame us?"
2. "Who resists His will?"
3. "Who are you, O man, to talk back to God?"
4. "Shall what is formed say to Him that formed it, 'Why did You make me like this?'"
5. "Does not the potter have the right to make out of the same lump of clay some pottery for noble purpose and some for common use?"
6. "What if God, choosing to show His wrath and make His power known, bore with great patience the objects of his Wrath— prepared for destruction?"
7. "What if He did this to make the riches of His glory known to the objects of His mercy, whom He prepared in advance for glory—even us, whom He also called, not only from the Jews, but also from the Gentiles?"

When Lee looked up, Ted pointed out, "The first question we've already answered as to how God can be fair and still demand us to do something He has hardened us not to do. From what we've learned already, the answer to the second question is that anybody who's alive and has ordinary intelligence can resist His will.

"The metaphorical questioner in question 3 asks, 'Who are you, O man, to talk back to God?' He wants to know what right do mere humans have to talk back to God or to resist His will. So do we have the right to resist God's commands?"

"We couldn't," Lee inserted, "if He had predestined us by divine fiat."

"Or we could if God had granted us the ability to make free will choices at the time of our creation," Tom quickly retorted.

"I think that Fast Draw McGraw, Tom, is right," Ted announced. "But neither of Tom's nor Lee's responses cancels out the other. That's because each conclusion depends on the correctness of a prior foundation—are human choices predestined, or are they made by free will?"

Thinking out loud, Bob noted, "This means that either answer to the third question could be correct, depending on which of the prior foundations is valid. Up to now, however, I thought that our objective was to discover which one is correct."

"It still is, Bob," Ted noted. "However, even though Paul is taking his time in getting us there, I think we'll arrive at a conclusion soon. So, Barbara, will you read us the fourth question?"

"Sure, Ted, it's 'Why did You make me like this?'"

"Now we've arrived at the 'why' question, haven't we? So at the time of the creation, God must have asked Himself which would give Him the most satisfaction—humans who had to love Him because He had predestined them so they could make no other choice or humans who could make uncoerced free will choices based on observing His love for them and the fairness of how they had been treated."

"Ted, the answer to this problem of God was discussed thoroughly during our first session," Bill pointed out. "It's obvious that God would want our respect for Him to be voluntary."

"Thank you, Bill." Pausing for a moment to see if anyone disagreed before proceeding, Ted asked Kathy to read the fifth question.

Clearing her voice, she started. "Does not the potter have the right to make out of the same lump of clay some pottery for noble purpose and some for common use?"

"See, Ted!" Lee exclaimed. "This question makes it clear to me that all the previous questions were actually building a valid foundation for the doctrine of predestination and not a basis for free will as you have tried to promote."

"Well, Lee, I agree that all the previous questions could promote predestination if you approach them with an *a priori* mind-set aimed in that direction. However, now that we've been exposed to your belief, please help me understand how you view the components in this analogy of the potter. In your opinion, does the potter represent God?"

"Yes."

"And that the clay represents us humans. Right?"

"Yes."

"Then I suppose you believe that the pottery, made for noble use, represents those whom God has predestined to eternal life?"

"Yes."

"And what about the pots made for common use. Do they represent people who have been eternally damned?"

"Yes."

"Then, in your opinion, do you believe that once God had finished creating a given vessel, its outcome would be forever fixed?"

"Yes."

"If that's the case, then what use would God's mercy have on the pots (people) that He had made to be damned? Or what good would His grace have on those vessels (people) predestined for eternal life? And aren't there many places in scripture where God, through His prophets, urged people to turn from their evil ways? If the people, represented in the analogy of the potter and the clay, could not change their outcomes, why would God beg them to turn from their evil ways? Could not the pottery made for noble use represent Old Testament prophets or New Testament apostles who had been called to lead common (pots) people, like you and me, away from evil to God?"

Lee remained silent for a time as he realized his dilemma.

Then Pauline, with a hint of mischievousness in her voice, interrupted the discussion. "Ted, I thought for a moment that you were going to exceed Paul in asking a series of questions. But my anxiety was reduced when you stopped with only five."

Her observation relieved the tension as everyone, except Lee, began to laugh.

Then just before some less than congratulatory remarks could be hurled his way, the thought came to Lee that Paul's sixth question might turn things around. So looking up, he innocently asked, "Ted, may I read question 6?"

"Have at it, Lee," Ted said with a confident sound in his voice, as well as a look on his face betraying the same attitude.

A little miffed by Ted's look, Lee began. "What if God, choosing to show His wrath and make His power known, bore with great patience the objects of His wrath—prepared for destruction?"

With a slight air of renewed assurance, Lee commented, "See, the objects of God's wrath have been prepared for destruction. This proves that they had been predestined for this outcome."

"Lee, God's patience bore long with the pharaoh and the Egyptians before they were destroyed in the Red Sea. If they had been predestined for this fate, why would He remain patient with them for the first five plagues?"

"Ted, it's because of what happens in question 7."

"Go ahead, Lee, and read that one to us."

"Okay, here it is. 'What if He did this to make the riches of His glory known to the objects of His mercy, whom He prepared in advance for glory—even us, whom he also called, not only from the Jews, but also from the Gentiles?'

"See, Ted, the objects of His mercy also had been prepared or predestined 'in advance for glory.'"

"But, Lee, did you notice that the words **objects** and **us** are both plural and that God had **called** them? If each one of them previously had been predestined for eternal life, why would God need to **call** them or show mercy to them when they already would have been predestined for eternal life? Each person had been called, but only those who choose to stop rebelling and join God's chosen people, the group forming God's invisible church, the group that He had predestined before the foundation of the world, could be saved. And let me also point out that those individuals who chose to remain in rebellion formed the group that God predestined for damnation. However, God didn't need to know what their choices were going to be until after they were made."

Reluctantly, Lee admitted that he had no answer to what Ted had pointed out.

With his admission, everyone was quiet for a few moments as they realized that basically Lee just had conceded that Calvin's understanding of predestination was flawed.

Loran broke the silence with an observation. "I think Paul, in verses 30-32, puts to rest Calvin's notion of predestination, which he tried to derive from previous verses in Romans 9. Paul asks another question, 'What then shall we say?' This time he answers it with a conclusion. The Gentiles had obtained righteousness by faith in what God was able to do through Jesus with their sinful lives, whereas the Hebrews had tried to obtain righteousness by keeping the law. Paul mentions nothing about God creating two divisions of people, some to be saved and some to be damned. Those who were saved obtained their righteousness by faith, whereas those who didn't had stumbled over Christ, a figurative stumbling stone. This occurred when they rejected Him. Paul finally summarizes the whole gospel in Romans 10:9-10, where he says, 'That if you confess with your mouth, Jesus is Lord, and believe in your heart that God raised him from the dead, you will be saved.' This is the simple gospel that Paul undoubtedly had preached in the outback of Asia Minor, and now, in this letter, he finally announces to the Christians in Rome."

"Whew, that's such a simple summary of the gospel," Carole said aloud. "I'm glad for this conclusion."

"And so am I," Lee finally admitted. "Now I won't have to wonder if I was created to be among the blessed or the damned. With the Spirit's prompting, I can choose where I want to spend eternity."

"Janice, can we go home now?" someone asked.

"Of course."

But before dismissing the group, she announced that next week's topic is going to be about how prophecy is connected to man's free will. Loran already has agreed to preside over this study, so Ted and Lee wouldn't be debating.

"That's a relief," Bill muttered under his breath as they all began to leave.

Summary of Chapter Three

1. Calvin claims that before God created every intelligent being, both human and angelic, He "appoints some to eternal life and others to eternal damnation." This is known as double predestination.

2. Calvin's teaching that God, before creation, predestined some intelligent beings to eternal life and others to eternal perdition is heretical as far as true Christianity is concerned. First, predestination made God the originator of all evil in the universe, when He created the first person that He had created to sin. Second, it completely nullifies the gospel, making the life, death, and resurrection of Jesus of no avail, since each one's eternal destination already had been decided by God Himself before their individual creation.

3. Modern-day Christians who believe they have been saved and adhere to Calvin's teachings on double predestination use it as a kind of "get out of jail free" card. God can't send them to perdition because they think they have been predestined to eternal life. Those predestined to eternal damnation can't help it. They were predestined that way by God.

4. The doctrine of double predestination brings up the question of how could any intelligent created being choose to love or fear God if all choices regarding their relationship to God had resulted from a capricious divine decision made before they even existed?

5. The opposite also would be true for God. How could He love any intelligent being if He had created each one to love or fear Him when they had no choice in the matter?

6. Predestination, as taught by Calvin, plays havoc with both God's mercy and His grace. There was no way He could show any individual mercy or grace since, according to Calvin, God already had decided by divine fiat where every individual was going to spend eternity.

Chapter Four

Prophecy and Man's Free Will

At the outset of the next meeting, Hank asked Loran, in jest, "Will you allow Ted or Lee to take over your lead in our study of man's free will versus prophecy as they have done in our last three sessions?"

Pausing for a moment and clearing his throat, Loran replied, "I'll try not to let that happen again. I don't, however, want the two of them to feel like they can't participate in this, a similar topic. We'll have to wait and see."

By this time, everyone had found a place to sit, so Loran, with a slight payback in his voice, asked Hank to lead the group in prayer.

Hank, sheepishly, bowed his head with the others and asked God to enlighten their minds as they took up the study of the relationship between Bible prophecy and man's free will.

Loran, from a few prepared notes, began his presentation. "First, we need to understand that at least three different categories of Biblical prophecies exist.

> "*Category I Prophecies* are fulfilled by God when He acts totally independent of mankind.

> "*Category II Prophecies* are fulfilled by God at some future time as inevitable results of human choices, usually with God intervening along the way.

> "*Category III Prophecies* fulfillment occurs when God promises that He will act in a certain way depending on choices made by a person or a group of people. This kind

of prophecy occasionally is combined with *Categories I and II.*"

"Will you cite examples of each?" Hank interrupted.

"Yes, Hank," Loran said. "As an example of a *Category I* is the second coming of Jesus. When God the Father decides that the time has come, it will happen. Even though the prediction of the second coming, made two thousand years ago, is attached to many preceding signs, some of which are the result of human free will choices, it doesn't mean that these signs are the cause of the second coming and Judgment Day. That day will occur when God decides."

"But that hasn't happened yet. Maybe it never will," Linda commented. "How about citing a *Category I* prophecy that has already come to pass?"

Putting his notes down and turning toward Linda, Loran said, "The first coming of Jesus should suffice as an example. Apostle Paul, writing to the Galatians, said in chapter 4, verse 4, 'But when the time had fully come, God sent his son, born of a woman, born under the law, to redeem those under the law, that we might receive the full rights of sons.'"

"According to this source, something happened, but had this event been predicted a significant time before it came to pass?" Linda questioned again.

"You're putting Loran on the spot," Janice interjected.

"It's okay, Janice, I think I can answer Linda's question. Read the whole Isaiah 53, which predicted the birth of a redeemer written several hundred years before Christ's birth. Then we have the predictions that Angel Gabriel made to Mary regarding the Christmas story fulfilled shortly thereafter. These are only two of many that I could cite."

Before Loran could pick up his notes, Pat raised her hand and began to talk. "Recently, I read the text you cited from Galatians to a friend, who responded by saying, 'Isn't this a little chauvinistic since only sons receive rights?'"

"Your friend seemed to forget that it was a woman, not a man, who gave birth to Jesus. Note too that the word 'we,' which, in this case, includes both male and female genders, shows that all can 'receive the full rights of sons.'"

Loran resumed where he had left off. "An example of a *Category II Prophecy* is the story of Joseph. His tragic removal, at age seventeen, from his family by his jealous brothers was an attempt on their part to remove him forever from their presence. However, many years before this injustice occurred, God predicted to Abraham (Joseph's great-grandfather) that his (Abraham's) descendants would live as sojourners in Egypt for about four hundred years. God could have fulfilled this prediction in various ways. But He used a famine and Joseph to bring this about.

"To recap briefly: When the opportunity arose, Joseph's jealous brothers sold him to a caravan of Ishmaelite merchants on their way to Egypt. They, in turn, sold him into Egyptian slavery. Potiphar, a government official, bought Joseph, intending to use him as a house boy. In this milieu, Joseph soon learned the culture and language of the Egyptians. Potiphar later discovered that Joseph could handle business matters very well. He made him overseer of all that he had. Under Joe's management, Potiphar became rich.

"Meanwhile, as the years passed, Joe, probably in his mid-twenties, had matured into a good-looking young man, who did not go unnoticed by Potiphar's wife. Joe repeatedly resisted her romantic advances. Angered by Joseph's rejection, she lied to her husband about Joseph one day, when Potiphar returned home from work.

"She said, 'Your Hebrew slave attempted to rape me but retreated when I screamed.'

"Potiphar threw him into the slammer, but Joe soon rose to the position of the chief warden, even though a prisoner himself. More years passed. Through the interpretation of the pharaoh's dream, a providential event, Joseph suddenly found himself, at age thirty, out of prison and prime minister of Egypt. In addition, he was charged with the care of a booming economy with seven years of bumper crops ahead. According to the pharaoh's dream, this time of plenty was to be followed by seven years of famine. Pharaoh gave Joseph authority to collect, as a tax, one-fifth of the grain produced during each of the seven years of plenty. Joseph had huge granaries built to store the excess wheat.

"As predicted, the seven fat years were followed by seven lean years and famine. To meet the needs for food, Joseph sold the grain back to the Egyptians for money. When their money ran out, the people traded their livestock for food. When the people had no more livestock, they sold their land and finally themselves for sustenance. The pharaoh became fabulously wealthy.

"Meanwhile, in the land of Canaan, where Joseph's family lived, the famine had spread, and his family was starving. When they heard that grain was for sale in Egypt, his brothers traveled there to buy grain. Later, at Joe's insistence, the whole family moved to Egypt, where they lived for about four hundred thirty years, fulfilling the prophecy made to Abraham more than four hundred years before.

"The famine in Canaan, combined with plenty of food in Egypt, caused the Israelites to immigrate to Egypt. Only then could Joseph tell his brothers, 'But God sent me ahead of you to preserve for you a remnant on earth and to save your lives by a great deliverance.' (Genesis 45:7, NIV)

"This is an example of a *Category II Prophecy* that became fulfilled at a future time as the direct result of many human freewill choices, with God obviously intervening along the way."

Loran hesitated momentarily at the end of telling Joseph's story, and John, thinking out loud, muttered, "I've heard that the historicity of this story is in question."

To that remark, Loran quickly responded. "I can see why you, as someone employed as an IRS tax collector, would find this story of Joseph hard to believe. First, he had a mandate from the pharaoh, by which he collected one-fifth of the grain production for seven years straight. This excess farm commodity he stored in government warehouses. When the famine came, he sold the product back to the very people whose work had produced it in the first place. It's a tax collector's dream come true."

After the group had stopped laughing, Loran took up where he had left off. "An example of a *Category III Prophecy* is the story of Jonah and Nineveh, a conditional prophecy. Destruction of the city of Nineveh depended upon whether or not people of that city chose to repent. When God saw that they truly did repent and turn from their evil ways, He had compassion and did not destroy them as He had threatened." (Jonah 3:10)

Phillip raised his hand, and after Loran nodded, Phil indicated that Loran had left out the most important part of the story. "As a kid, if I remember the Sunday-school lesson correctly, Jonah fell off the boat when this one big fish jerked on his fishing line. Once in the water, the critter swallowed him in one gulp, along with a hook, line, and sinker."

With a big grin, Loran responded. "You got a portion of the story right. Actually, the sailors threw Jonah overboard in a storm to save themselves and the ship. The fish then swallowed Jonah whole. Aside from the conditional prophecy, this story from the Bible is also one of the best to show how God responds to a series of human freewill choices."

"I've always heard this saga referred to as Jonah and the whale," remarked Barbara.

"Yeah, and I heard that whales don't have throats big enough to swallow a man whole," Heather noted.

"How could the stomach of this critter have enough air in it to keep Jonah alive for three days and three nights?" questioned Annie.

"Wouldn't the enzymes digest a man?" inquired Howard.

"Give Loran at least a second to answer!" shouted Gayle.

Pausing for a moment to gather his wits, Loran responded. "First of all, the text says that God had prepared a big fish to swallow Jonah alive. God did not get caught off guard. He had the fish ready ahead of time with everything needed to keep Jonah alive inside. Regardless, it couldn't have been a whale because they are mammals and not fish. We've gotten ahead of the story, so let's get back to the beginning and see how God is always prepared to respond to all our freewill choices. As Bill pointed out to us a week or two back, God doesn't need to know what every human freewill choice is going to be before it is made for Him to have His response ready. From His vantage point, God can see every possible freewill choice available for any person to make in any given situation. He knows in advance what His response will be for every choice possible, similar to how a master chess player operates."

"Jonah apparently had heard how cruel and mean the people of Nineveh were to anyone they captured, so he was afraid to go there and preach destruction against that city and its inhabitants. The story of Jonah involves an example of a *Category III Bible Prophecy*, the fulfillment of which, was predicated on how the people of Nineveh might choose to respond to Jonah's preaching. But it is also an example of how God is sometimes able to 'persuade' people to make choices He wants them to make. Let's see how God got Jonah to change his mind so this particular prophecy could come to pass.

God's Algorithm of Responses to Jonah's Freewill Choices

God said to Jonah, "Go to Nineveh and preach against it." (Jonah 1:2)

Besides going to Nineveh, Jonah had numerous other freewill choices.

He could refuse, beg God to send another man, run
to Egypt, sail to Tarshish or commit suicide.

Jonah chose a boat to sail to Tarshish. (Jonah 1:3)

God responded with a storm. (Jonah 1:4)

Jonah chose assisted suicide to save the ship and crew.
They threw him overboard. (Jonah 1:15)

God responded by having a great fish prepared to swallow
Jonah. He was in the belly of the fish for three days and three
nights, where he did a lot of thinking. (Jonah 1:17)

Jonah finally chose to pray to God from inside the fish. (Jonah 2:1-9).

God responded by having the fish vomit
Jonah onto dry land. (Jonah 2:10)

God told Jonah the second time to Go to Nineveh. (Jonah 3:1)

This time Jonah chose to go and preach against the city. (Jonah 3:3)

The city was saved when the people humbled
themselves before God. (Jonah 3:10)

Jonah expressed disappointment with God
because God was merciful. (Jonah 4)

"We don't know how God would have responded to Jonah if he
had chosen one of the other possibilities, but we know that He always
was prepared to respond appropriately to any possible choice Jonah
might have made. We know what happened to Moses when he begged

God to send someone else. We know what happened to Elijah when he headed toward Egypt but got stopped in Sinai. And we know what happened to Balaam when God told him not to go someplace, but he went nevertheless."

Hank broke in just then, saying, "This story reminds me of some Bible prophecies regarding certain individuals whom I heard about in Sunday school when I was a kid. As I recall, some predictions of certain men were described in detail before their birth. If the principles regarding man's free will are true, I wonder how God could predict what the activities of men with free will are going to be prior to being born. If He can't know for sure what choices men are going to make before they occur, how can He make prophecies like these?"

Bill spoke up just then. "Loran just showed us that God knows ahead of time every possible choice available to a person in each situation and what His immediate response will be to any given choice that a person can make."

"But the situation I'm talking about is different," Hank interrupted. "I can understand that God can foresee all the freewill choices available to a person in any given circumstance and can be ready for His best response to any choice that a person makes. In the fulfillment of those kinds of prophecies, however, God is dealing with a person and a situation that already exists. But what I'm talking about are prophecies that God made of individuals several generations before their existence. So how could God predict that a specific person would even exist hundreds of years before his birth, much less what choices he was going to make? To me, there seems to be too many variables that remain unknown, even to God, for fulfillment of these prophecies."

Just then, Gary, a history buff, entered the discussion. "Along the same line, I heard about one Old Testament prophecy regarding Cyrus, one of the kings of Persia. (Isaiah 44:28) Prophet Isaiah made the prediction many years before the birth of this king. The prophecy not only called him by name, but also predicted that he would decree that the Jews return to Jerusalem and rebuild the temple. To my way of thinking, if this is true, God knows a lot of histories in advance by divine fiat. But this calls into question the freedom of men making freewill choices, doesn't it?"

"Yes, that's how I see this situation," commented Howard. "Unless all the people involved in Cyrus' ancestry were foreknown to God and existed by His divine commands, how could He have Isaiah speak with such specificity, both as to the predicted name of the king and what his actions would be?"

"That's what I was thinking exactly," Phyllis interrupted. "Without God's command, how could God know all those years in advance that a boy would be born to a mother who would name him Cyrus? Later, when he became king of Persia, how could God know that Cyrus would order the Israelites back to Jerusalem?"

Loran responded without looking at his notes. "This is an example of a *Category II Prophecy* that we talked about earlier. With these prophecies, God intervenes all along the way by bringing pressure on people to make the choices He wants them to make. This way, the predicted prophecy will come true. These prophecies result from a combination of human choices and God's intervention. God has a myriad ways to get people to change their minds. For example, let's go back to the story of Jonah.

"As I mentioned earlier, he had heard about the atrocities committed by the people of Nineveh against their captives and decided that he wasn't going there regardless of what God told him to do. He was so afraid of being tortured that he chose to flee as far away from Nineveh as he could get. But God caused a storm to rock the boat so hard that the sailors threw him overboard, and God prepared a fish to swallow His stubborn prophet. But Jonah was so afraid of Ninevehite torture that it took him three days and three nights in the belly of the fish with seaweed wrapped around his head (Jonah 2:5) before he figured that the torture in Nineveh could be no worse than being digested alive and excreted as fish feces or, worse yet, a big fish flatus. It was then that he prayed for deliverance and was expelled in a bolus of vomit onto dry land. Then when God told him again to go to Nineveh, he went of his own choice.

"Even though this part of the story doesn't involve the original prophecy, this is an example of how God can 'persuade' people to change their freewill minds for a prophecy to be fulfilled. The example of Jonah is an extreme way that God used to put pressure on some folks to get them to change their freewill minds. He also has many milder methods to get people to change their minds. Regardless, people can always refuse. If they do, God can get His prophecy fulfilled by turning to someone else. That's how God can predict, years ahead of time, what someone will name their child and what that child will grow up to do."

Bob, who had missed the previous meeting, interrupted the discussion. "I distinctly recall one of my Sunday school teachers reading from someplace in the New Testament, I believe from the book of Romans, about God predicting from His foreknowledge the adult actions of two unborn twins. From this example, I was told that God knows what I'm going to do before I do it. So, Loran, what do you think of this?"

"Bob, it doesn't matter what I think," Loran responded. "Too bad you missed last week's session, when we discussed this prophecy in detail. Maybe we should ask Ted to go over this prophecy with us again. Will this be okay with you, Hank, and the rest of you?"

"Sure, Loran," several said, including Hank.

Ted, with a slight reluctance, began. "We find this passage in Romans 9:10-24 (NIV). But before I read it, let me give a little background to this Old Testament story. Rebecca, Isaac's wife, was pregnant with twins, and they were jostling each other around in her womb. Apparently, this worried her so much that 'she went to inquire of the Lord' and was told the following as recorded in Genesis 25:23 (NIV): 'Two nations are in your womb, and two peoples from within you will be separated; one people will be stronger than the other, and the older will serve the younger.' This prophecy has three components. Progenitors of two peoples were in Rebecca's womb. One would be stronger than the other, and the older would serve the younger.

"With this, let me read what Apostle Paul said about this prophecy Romans 9:10-13 (NIV): 'Yet, before the twins were born or had done anything good or bad-in order that God's purpose in election might stand: not by works but by him who calls-she was told, "the older will serve the younger." Just as it is written: "Jacob I loved, but Esau I hated. "

"Much later, after their births, without violating man's free will, God could work things out just as He did with Joseph, so that each of these non-identical twins would become a progenitor of a people and, thereby, form two great nations. By God's election (or choice), He could know that thousands of years later, through His divine interventions, Jesus would be born in Jacob's genetic line, causing his nation to be the strongest. This made Esau, the elder twin, subservient to Jacob, the younger. From His plan, God could know this before either child had done 'anything good or bad.'

61

"Without careful reading, the next sentence ("Jacob I loved, but Esau I hated") sounds like God began hating the firstborn twin and loving the second-born while they were still in the womb. Notice that the words, placed in the past tense, were taken from the last Old Testament book quoted from Malachi 1:2-3 (NIV). They were written about a thousand years later than the time of Rebecca's travail. Malachi called each nation by the names of their respective predecessors. This scripture did not mean that God decided by divine election that He loved one unborn baby and hated the other. Rather, it was how the two brothers had individually responded to God's leading in each of their lives that caused Him, hundreds of years later, to hate one nation and love the other.

"Bob, I have to disagree with the conclusion that your Sunday school teacher drew from this story. God has a thousand ways to have His prophecies fulfilled without violating man's free will."

Bob was quiet for a few moments before speaking. "Thanks, Ted, for this explanation. This has bothered me for a long time."

"You can see from these Old Testament examples," Loran pointed out, "that God has various means at His disposal to place pressure on people to get them to change their minds, but in the end, God honors man's free will."

"Loran," Tom broke in, "that was a great review that Ted gave us, and I thank him as did Bob, but does this mean that God could place enough pressure on everybody causing them to change their minds so that no one will go to hell?"

"No, Tom," Loran responded. "If that were the case, then God would become responsible for preventing everyone from going to that place. Anyone who goes to hell, however, will go there because of their own freewill choice."

"But, Loran," Tom interrupted again, "I've always been taught that God lets good people into heaven and throws bad people into hell."

"Well, Tom, remember what we learned in one of our previous sessions? Goodness from God's perspective is always founded on unconditional love and unselfishness, both of which are always demonstrated by acts of choosing to place others first and ourselves last. On the other hand, evil is the exact opposite—always being based on the choice of placing oneself first and others last. This concept is illustrated very well by disobeying any one of the Ten Commandments. When violating any of the first four, we place ourselves above God, and when disobeying any of the last six, we put ourselves above our fellow man. Therefore, breaking any one is a selfish act. In fact, when we willfully disobey God, we think that we know better than He. This choice is the most prideful selfish act there is and forms the basis for every kind of evil or sin that exists. It is always destructive to oneself and to others as well. Therefore, all sin is nothing more than a camouflaged form of self-destruction. We are all inherently selfish, which means that subconsciously, we place ourselves above everyone else, including God and our fellow man.

"Conversely, any form of goodness involves placing others first and ourselves last. Unselfishness is a disguised form of love and is constructive. It builds up its possessor and those impacted by it as well. But don't forget, all forms of good or evil are only powerless concepts, unable to exist independent of an intelligent mind, which chooses to judge and act between the two. Hell is the ultimate place where God allows people who choose to persist in selfishness to go to self-destruct."

Carolyn broke into the discussion just then by asking, "I heard one preacher say that belief in Jesus will prevent a person from going to Hell. But how could Jesus be part of the eternal Trinity if He was born as God's son, when all three are supposed to be eternal?"

"Whew, this is a tough question," Loran responded. "I'll see what I can do. According to John (John 1:1-3), Jesus has always existed in an incarnate form, as part of the Godhead. He became God's earthly son, and God became His heavenly Father when they chose to have Jesus born in human form on this earth, confined in the same carbon-based life He had created in the first place. This was a very unselfish act on the part of Jesus, only to be exceeded when He allowed Himself to be crucified on a cross in our place. His substitutionary death for us would have had no meaning, however, if Jesus had not been part of the Godhead or if He had committed one selfish act. His life lived unselfishly proved how Adam and Eve could have lived. Instead of believing God, they believed the serpent's lies that they would not die and would become as wise as God if they ate the fruit. They placed the serpent's lies above God's truth, a very selfish act. To reverse what the original human pair did, we have to do just the opposite. Disbelieve the serpent, believe in Jesus, and with the help of the Holy Spirit, begin to live unselfishly. Then we will not self-destruct in hell.

"The act of crucifying Jesus shows just how destructive human selfishness and hatred had become. First, we disbelieved God. Then we ate some forbidden fruit, the initial human act of selfishness. Then over time, selfish traits grew in the human race to the point of participating in the murder of Jesus, a member of the Trinity, confined in flesh. The men at the time believed they were doing humanity a favor by trying to rid the world of a man who claimed that unselfish love for others was the only way to live. However, it was not the attempts of these selfish men to kill Jesus. He died when the Father separated from Him. Jesus cried out, 'My God, my God, why have you forsaken Me?' (See Matthew 27:46.).

"In reality, this was the supreme example of mankind's destructive hate. It caused us to try to murder Jesus, the sustainer of our lives, without whom we would perish. (Colossians 1:15-17 and Hebrews 1:3, NIV) But paradoxically, Jesus' death paved the way for God to forgive us for all the times we have indulged in hatred and self-destruction. The terrible scene of the crucifixion causes some of us to turn away in disgust, realizing that placing others first in love is the only right way to live. When this realization finally sinks into our feeble minds, we are born again. We have moved from death to life. (John 3:1-16 and John 5:24, NIV) We are declared righteous and justified in God's sight, caused by nothing we did except to make an unselfish choice. Pride is cast aside with the realization that there is no work we can do to rectify our position with God because Jesus did it already. No matter how selfish and hateful a person we may have been in the past, our repentance brings forgiveness. This occurs when we realize that Jesus died in our place. Our selfish, hateful life is exchanged for Christ's unselfish, loving life. (2 Corinthians 5:21, NIV)

"After our justification before God has taken place, selfishness and hatred are not instantly abolished from our lives. Our conscience forces us to repent again and again for our hateful, selfish acts, which frequently well up within us. With the help of God's Spirit, these traits are slowly removed from our daily living. This process is called sanctification and is hard work. It will never be completed this side of Jesus' second coming. (Philippians 1:6) But no matter how much progress we make, this work does not improve our position with God. This is because, in both our justification and sanctification, we are completely dependent on His mercy and grace. As we've learned, mercy is not getting the inevitable result that our selfishness deserves, and grace is getting the reward that we don't. When life as we know it ends, this is how God will look at those, who, with their free wills, have chosen love over hate. This choice, Carolyn, is what prevents our entrance into hell."

"Wow, Loran!" Kathy nearly shouted. "You should have been a preacher. That's the best short sermon I've ever heard. I hesitate to remind you of your saying that Romans 10 makes these things very short. So is the gospel presented there even shorter than what you just taught us?"

"It is very short. Let me read just two verses from Romans 10:9-10: 'That if you confess with your mouth, Jesus is Lord, and believe in your heart that God raised him from the dead, you will be saved. For it is with your heart that you believe and are justified, and it is with your mouth that you confess and are saved.'"

"Loran," Kathy said and loudly again, "that was short and also easy to remember."

It seemed that the session was about to close as several gathered their things and stood up.

So turning to Janice, Gary mused, "I wonder if there are any scientists who have given their opinions as to whether or not free will exists in the human psyche?"

"And I'd like to know what science has to say about evil," Annie broke in.

Janice indicated that she didn't know what science had to say about either subject, so she quickly bounced these questions off Ted, who was standing nearby. "Do you know if anyone in the scientific community has ventured into these specializations?"

"Yes, I've heard of some. I'll see what I can find."

"Great!" Janice exclaimed. "That will be your assignment. Would you give a report of your findings at our next meeting?"

"I'll try, Janice."

"Okay, you're on." With that, she dismissed the meeting.

Summary of Free Will and Bible Prophecies

1. *Category I Prophecies* are fulfilled by God when He acts totally independent of mankind.
2. *Category II Prophecies* are fulfilled by God at some future time as inevitable results of human choices, usually with God intervening along the way.

3. *Category III Prophecies* are fulfilled when God promises that He will act in a certain way depending on choices made by a person or a group of people. This kind of prophecy occasionally is combined with *Categories I and II.*

4. The first and second comings of Jesus are examples of *Category I Prophecies.*

5. The story of Joseph exemplifies a *Category II Prophecy.*

6. An example of a *Category III Prophecy* is the story of Jonah and Nineveh.

7. The story of Jonah involves an example of a *Category III Prophecy*, the fulfillment of which was predicated on how the people of Nineveh might choose to respond to Jonah's preaching. But it is also an example of how God is sometimes able to "persuade" people to make choices He wants them to make.

8. The story of conversion of the people of the city of Nineveh is an example of how God, through the preaching of Jonah, was able to get a whole city of people to change their ways. At the outset of the story, it is easy to believe that the majority of people in that city had been predestined to perdition. However, from the outcome of Jonah's prophetic preaching of oncoming doom, it is easy to see that at least hundreds, if not thousands, changed their positions. The conversion from their evil ways to the right goes a long way toward showing that Calvin's brand of predestination is bogus.

9. Though God, in many instances, can influence free will to His liking, in the end, He allows each individual's free will to dictate how that person chooses to react in each situation.

Chapter Five

Science and Man's Free Will

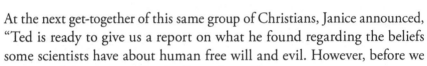

At the next get-together of this same group of Christians, Janice announced, "Ted is ready to give us a report on what he found regarding the beliefs some scientists have about human free will and evil. However, before we get started, let me pray for God's guidance."

When Janice finished praying, Ted passed around a handout he had compiled regarding human free will and evil and what some scientists think about these two subjects.

As the handouts were being passed, he started speaking. "I made enough copies for each of you to follow along as we read. But before we learn what some scientists think regarding free will and evil, we need to learn about four divisions of evil that Hugh Sylvester described in his book *Arguing with God*.[1] He divided evil, from the Judeo-Christian perspective, into two main categories—moral evil and natural evil, each of which he further divided into two. Please look at the first page of the handout, which shows Sylvester's outline. Understanding these divisions of evil will help us obtain a clearer perception of the thinking and opinions of several men of science regarding their views of human free will and its relationship to evil.

I. Moral Evil

- Evil A: The rebellion of man against God
- Evil B: The ill-treatment of man by man

II. Natural Evil

- Evil C: Those evils that come from the disease-death environment, catastrophic events such as earthquakes, inhospitable regions of the earth (e.g., those with low rainfall).
- Evil D: Animal pain and suffering, which possibly includes the case of idiot children. The whole natural order of 'the survival of the fittest.'"

After everyone had a chance to look over the outline, Ted said, "Many Judeo-Christians understand the Bible teaches that the rebellion against God, noted in the handout, as one kind of moral evil, started in heaven. Apparently, it first arose as a freewill choice in Lucifer's mind. He was one of God's holy angels. **See Isaiah 14:12-14 and Ezekiel 28:11-19.** Second, it spread to one-third of the other angels. **(Revelation 1:20, 12:4 and 9)** Then war in heaven resulted. Lucifer, later known as Satan, along with his angels, was cast out of heaven to this earth, and thus, all evil in the entire universe was confined to this planet. **(Revelation 12:7-9)** Even though mankind was made in the image of God and pronounced good by their Creator, Satan extended his rebellion against God to humans with a subtle, deceptive choice." **(Genesis 3)**

Ted then read from the handout. "According to **Genesis 3**, after Adam and Eve chose to believe the serpent instead of God, their rebellion introduced moral evil into the human race. God drove them out of the garden because the rebels could not be allowed to eat 'from the Tree of Life and . . . live forever.' **(Genesis 3:22)** Death for mankind was required as one way to slow down evil's reign on humanity until God could stomp on the serpent's head and destroy evil forever without being seen as a tyrant.

"Their rebellious choice rested on the beguiling voice of the serpent who said, 'You will not surely die.' This lie was followed by 'For God knows that when you eat of it your eyes will be opened, and you will be like God, knowing good and evil.' Believing Satan instead of God, coupled with selfish pride, enhanced by a desire to become wise like God, enticed them to rebel against Him. Their rebellion introduced mankind to part A of moral evil. Part B, man's ill-treatment of man, was only a short step beyond his rebellion against God, as witnessed by the story of Cain and Abel. Without access to the Tree of Life, part C of natural evil could begin. Painful childbirth for women and tough work for men followed with each being accompanied by suffering, disease, and death. However, the timing of part D of natural evil preceded part C. Animal suffering occurred right away, when skins were used to provide clothing for the naked, primordial pair.

"Now with an understanding of moral evil and natural evil firmly in mind, we'll soon be ready to understand the relationship that science espouses between free will and evil, pain and suffering. Before we go there, however, we need to consider something else that Hugh Sylvester describes in his book. So, Janet, would you read the next paragraph from the handout?"

Answering with an affirmative nod, Janet began reading with her distinct voice.

> Humans, as well as God, have first and second orders of approval for many situations. For instance, Mr. Sylvester shows us that humans have first-order approval of steak knives when used for eating steaks, but second-order approval of steak knives when used to commit murder. Just because a steak knife is rarely used for murder doesn't mean that humans throw all steak knives away.[2] The Bible is replete with examples showing that God does not approve of many thoughts and/or actions of humans. But, on the other hand, it doesn't teach that He decrees all the atoms and molecules composing our bodies fly apart, if we think or do something that displays our rebellion against Him.

Annie broke in just then with a question. "But wouldn't the immediate eradication of rebellion have been a quick fix for God to get rid of the problem of evil in His universe?"

"At first glance, that would seem true, Annie," Ted responded. "However, as noted above, God, as well as humans, has first and second orders of approval for various human thoughts and actions. When he pronounced all things good at the end of the sixth day of creation, the condition of humanity existing at that time met with His first order of approval. After man's rebellion against God arose on planet Earth, this situation resulted in God's second order of approval."

"How could evil anywhere in God's universe meet with any degree of approval from Him?" inquired Karen.

"Well, Karen," Ted responded, "keep in mind, Lucifer, or Satan, initiated the rebellion against God in heaven, after which he was able to persuade one-third of the angels to join him. The other two-thirds, however, remained loyal to their Creator. If God had immediately annihilated Satan and the third of the angelic host who went along with him, the other two-thirds of the non-rebellious angels might have thought, *Maybe Satan was right. We have to serve God or die. Maybe there's no other choice, and we can't afford to test God to find out.* The same notion would have applied after the rebellion of Adam and Eve. Their immediate destruction would have resulted in the same conclusion by the angels who had not rebelled. In addition, if God had immediately annihilated Cain after he killed his brother Abel, fear of destruction also would have become the motivating factor for all humans to worship God."

"I think I understand what you're saying, Ted," Loran interjected. "If God's judgment against any form of rebellion was always meted out with immediate destruction, then many intelligent beings who had not participated in the rebellion might be inclined to obey God, prompted by fear and self-preservation rather than admiration for His having given them life, ruled by His love and justice. It is my opinion that the fear of impending doom should never be a reason to serve God."

"That's exactly why I left the church in which I grew up," Tom interrupted. "I got tired of the clergy trying to scare me into heaven by threatening me with hellfire."

"I've noticed," Howard interjected, "that all carbon-based life has an overwhelming, innate desire to preserve itself."

Temporarily choosing to ignore Tom's remarks and Howard's observation, Ted responded to Loran. "You're right, Loran, instead of destroying all forms of evil immediately, God lets it play out until all intelligent beings everywhere in the universe will be able to see that if evil is allowed to continue long enough, evil by itself will cause the destruction of everyone. **(Mark 13:20)** When all intelligent creatures understand that evil is self-destructive to its advocates, as well as those at whom it is directed, God can destroy with fire all forms of moral evil and natural evil with love and justice. He can do this without any of the non-rebellious angels or a repentant mankind thinking that they must serve God from fear of being destroyed."

"Ted, your description of a cleansing fire that destroys all forms of evil seems more reasonable and just!" Tom exclaimed. "It is the idea of being confined forever in the flames of hell that some preachers use as a means of trying to scare people into heaven, which I have found objectionable. If God is love, He wouldn't confine people forever in flames that do not consume. If He is just, He wouldn't mete out this kind of punishment when evil by itself would kill all the perpetrators, as well as those who aren't. I couldn't stand this preaching, so I left the church in which I was raised."

"Tom, there is more than one place in Revelation, the last book of the Bible, where descriptions of eternal fire seem to indicate that the flames never go out. However, **Jude verse 7,** in the book just before Revelation, says that the cities of Sodom and Gomorrah 'serve as an example of those who suffer the punishment of **eternal fire.**' And **2 Peter 2:6,** speaking of God, says the same thing: 'He condemned the cities of Sodom and Gomorrah by burning them to ashes, and made them an example of what is going to happen to the ungodly.' On a trip to the Holy Land, Tom, I observed that there is nothing burning at the former location of these cities. As I see it, God's eternal fire, though unquenchable, burns until whatever God meant for it to destroy is consumed."

Speaking in a louder voice than before, Howard said, "But I've noticed that all carbon-based life has an overwhelming, innate desire to preserve itself. Even a fly tries to escape the swatter."

Kathy, looking directly at him, said, "Thanks, Howard, for again pointing out this universal characteristic of carbon-based life. No matter the species, each tries to preserve its life and live as long as possible. This reminds me of what Mr. Sylvester said about natural evil and its relationship to the disease-death environment. So how does the evil of suffering from any disease form part of God's second order of approval, and is it God's will for people to be sick? Ted, because you were a doctor before your retirement, I would like your take on these matters."

"Yes, yes," said several others almost in unison. "Tell us, Ted, about how you dealt with this question in your practice of medicine."

"Okay," Ted responded. "But before going there, we must recall many instances mentioned in scripture where God used different forms of natural evil to accomplish His purposes. Sometimes He used illnesses, but in addition, God has used everything from floods, whirlwinds, earthquakes, famines, and even snake bites to accomplish His goals.

"God allowed Satan to rain down a multitude of various forms of natural evil on Job's family and his possessions. On Job, however, Satan chose very painful sores. (**Job 1-2**) God wanted to prove to Satan that there was one person who would remain faithful to Him, no matter what. At a later time, God caused ten plagues to fall on Egypt, but only the sixth one produced an illness of boils. However, it was the tenth plague of death that finally caused the pharaoh to allow the Israelites to leave Egypt. (**Exodus 7-11**) Another time when the ark of God was captured by the Philistines, He used a plague of hemorrhoids to influence the capturers of the ark to return it to the Israelites. (**1 Samuel 5-6**) God allowed Satan to cover Job with painful sores, but other times God produced the illnesses Himself.

"Excluding these times when God used some type of human misery to accomplish a specific goal, not all natural evil is produced by Him. Many human maladies result from man's freewill choices. Failure or refusal to follow rules of health, such as overeating, lack of exercise or rest, smoking, and misuse of alcohol, are common examples. Regardless, all kinds of natural evil tragedies, including those caused by earthquakes, storms, or devastating accidents, and even mental illnesses or babies born with some kind of defect, can be traced back to the wrong choices of Adam and Eve in the garden. But God is aware of the presence of every human tragedy. He uses each of them to stimulate in us a desire to exit from this environment of God's second order of approval to one with His first.

"Now with this brief introduction into various causes of natural evil, I'd like to tell you about my first confrontation with questions regarding suffering, disease, and evil and their relationship to free will. This occurred when I was a junior medical student at the 2,500-bed Los Angeles County Hospital. I happened to hear, by way of the medical student grapevine, about a patient who had been admitted with an extremely rare diagnosis known as Wilson's disease. This malady is caused by an inherited inborn error of metabolism for copper. If not treated, it, among other things, results in cirrhosis of the liver and death. One sign of this rare disease is a ring, varying in color from red, green, blue, yellow, or brown that develops in the cornea just inside of the limbus of each eye. They are known as Kayser-Fleischer rings and are visible at the bedside with the aid of an ordinary ophthalmoscope.

"As I was examining this patient's eyes, a thought came to me out of nowhere. *Why am I not in this patient's bed with his problem and he standing out here examining me? Why was he suffering and I was not?*

My first mental response, *it is God's will.* Then I suddenly realized, *If it was God's will and I was trying to learn how to help people with this condition, or any other illness for that matter, then I would be trying to undo something that God willed. I'd be fighting against God. But how could this be? Helping someone is an unselfish act. That can't possibly be against God. This conundrum forced me to think further.* Sylvester's book helped.

"This patient had inherited his deadly mutation from his parents, as an autosomal recessive disorder. This means that Wilson's disease can be expressed only in children of parents, each one of whom must be a carrier of this very rare mutation. Carriers don't have the disease themselves, but their genetic makeup is such that their offspring can inherit the actual disease from their genetic union. What are the odds out of millions that two people, each a carrier of this very rare mutation, just happened to meet, just happened to fall in love, just happened to marry, and just happened to procreate? They could not know that each of them carried the mutation in their genes, but their union unwittingly caused their son's illness. Because the patient could not choose his parents, it seemed to me that time and chance were active in this man's inheriting Wilson's disease."

"But, Ted, does God ever work with time and chance?" asked Nancy.

"Well, Nancy, in the past, I didn't think so. Then I read what King Solomon had to say about this subject in **Ecclesiastes 9:11**: 'The race is not to the swift or the battle to the strong, nor does food come to the wise or wealth to the brilliant or favor to the learned; but time and chance happen to them all.' So I thought, *Why couldn't time and chance be involved in the pathogenesis* (the origin and development) *of many diseases?*

"After reading what King Solomon said, I had to conclude that suffering and evil that all diseases produce, along with many other human miseries, sometimes can be caused by naturalistic forces, such as time and chance. They are not directly a product of God's will. This man's disease was simply another example of evil that God allows to persist as a second order of approval until He can destroy all forms of evil and not appear unjust.

"If God foreordains everything, and if He controls everything completely, including our choices, then the evil and suffering of Wilson's disease or any other malady will be the result of His divine fiat, making Him the originator of all human suffering and evil. On the other hand, if God foreknew while creating mankind that even one of them would

73

rebel against Him and if He willfully went ahead creating that person anyway, then God would become responsible for producing the first evil. This scenario also makes Him responsible for all of mankind's misery by creating a person that He knew beforehand would rebel and bring down a host of problems on the human race. If either of these situations is correct, then any person trying to help someone who is suffering or sick will find himself working against God.

"God is not the originator of evil and suffering but, instead, the originator of good. Anyone who tries to alleviate any human disease or suffering is not fighting against God or going against His will but rather is cooperating with Him. Together, they are beginning to return this planet back to His first order of approval. Activities such as preaching the gospel and healing physical maladies follow in the footsteps of Jesus. He came to reclaim this Earth from all forms of evil and return it to God's first order of approval.

"However, when God created all intelligent beings, including angels or humans with free will, He gave them the possibility to rebel, but not a mandate to do so. If humans with free will chose to rebel, then that choice would make mankind responsible for their part in the rebellion and God would remain innocent. However, the cause of every type of human suffering and evil can be traced back to mankind's original bad choice. Regardless, God can make 'all things work together for good,' even evil caused by time and chance."

"But why?" Kathy interrupted. "Why would God give us free will if He knew ahead of time that only one selfish choice would produce a lot of trouble?"

"All right, Kathy," Ted replied. "Let's recall what we learned at our very first get-together. Friendship and love for others should not depend totally on your feelings but, in addition, should be subservient to your will. True love always involves giving up some of your freedom, autonomy, and independence. When you love someone, at a minimum, a portion of your time must be devoted to them. Because you want to please the one you love, you must make choices that involve them as well as yourself. In short, since you don't know for sure how your loved one will accept your attempts at showing affection, you must be willing to place what you think you know about them on hold until you can see their response. You, thereby, have been willing, maybe unwittingly, to place your knowledge and your power to choose to be subservient to your loved one until that person makes a response. Freedom to love someone always comes with the risk of being rejected. Your heart may be broken in the process. That's a chance you must take, but when free will and feelings of both persons come together simultaneously, each obtains requited love.

"God's attempts to draw us back to Himself are no different. He shared small portions of His knowledge (**omniscience**) and power to choose (**omnipotence**) with us when He gave us free will. And just as we wait to see the response of a loved one to our amorous attempts, so also God waits to see ours. But in the end, as it is with any successful love, the loss of freedom and independence that each one voluntarily gives to the relationship is more than made up when each one receives love in return. Without freewill choices, agape love, which is unconditional and permanent, could not proceed from God to us, or from us to God, or from us to others. Each person, including God, 'Who first loved us,' must be able to make freewill choices.[3] When God created intelligent creatures with freewill, He took the same risk. He wanted to share His love with them and have them freely return love back to Him. The possibility for a bilateral loving response is the most important reason God gave angels and humans free will. Without free will, agape love could not exist.

"So, Annie, this is why God delays the destruction of all evil and rebellion. The postponement of evil's destruction forms His second order of approval, His **mercy.** He extends it for a time to all humans, regardless of whether or not they stop rebelling. Through repentance and forgiveness, God can bring every willing and repentant human rebel who chooses back to His first order of approval, through His **grace.** Though never deserved or earned, **grace** can be obtained only by believing in Jesus' redeeming life, sacrificial death, and resurrection. He waits to see our voluntary response to His agape love displayed toward us.

"Keep these notions of first and second orders of approval in mind as we continue to examine what suffering and death tell us about God. Remember, however, that all who end up in hellfire will be there as a result of each one's deliberate choice. They choose to maintain a selfish, prideful, rebellious stance and, thereby, attempt to place themselves above their fellow men and equal to, or even above, God.

"The hellfire kind of evangelism is based solely on the idea that every person wants to preserve their life. Fear of doom is not the primary reason to serve God. Rather, it should come from our gratitude and appreciation

vice versa. This discovery of the uncertainty principle was the beginning of quantum mechanics. The upstart of all this is that at the basic level of physical reality, not all identical causes have the same effect. Since our thoughts are nothing more than electrons and ions moving about in our brain cells, our thoughts cannot all be the result of previous random events over which we had no control. Quantum mechanics, which cannot totally predict the outcome of cause and effect at the subatomic level, should have sounded the death knell for the view that our thoughts have been prefixed (a psychological cemetery for its burial), but it hasn't. Our brains can produce original thoughts. We can change our minds, we do have free will, and we are responsible for our actions!"

Ted resumed reading from the handout.

> Provine is not the only scientist who espouses this notion of cognitive science. Melvin Konner, in the May 19, 2003, issue of *Nature* (pp. 17-18), expresses the same idea that the mind is "a survival machine with predetermined choices." He believes that free will is an illusion. Thomas W. Clark takes a similar stance in *Science and Consciousness Review*, May 2002, that free will is basically a self-deception.
>
> In the June 2014 issue of *Scientific American*, there appeared an article entitled "The World without Free Will" by Azim F. Shariff and Kathleen D. Vohs. They ask the question "What happens to a society that believes people have no conscious control over their actions?" In brief, they answer. In the past decade, an increasing number of neurologists and philosophers have argued that free will does not exist. Rather, we are pushed around by our unconscious minds, with the illusion of conscious control. In parallel, recent studies suggest that the more people doubt free will, the less they support criminal punishment and the less ethically they behave toward one another.
>
> In addition to the Heisenberg's uncertainty principle argument in favor of free will described above, the

January 2015 issue of *Scientific American* has an article by Eddy Nahmias titled "Why We Have Free Will." In it, Nahmias argues against other scientists who claim that human choices are an illusion and that we choose as "biochemical puppets. He calls them 'willusionists' due to the fact that the scientific evidence for their conclusions" fails to clearly define the border between conscious and unconscious actions. He goes on to find fault with the experiments that two of these willusionists use as proof against human free will. Nahmias proposes future experiments, which might prove whether or not that free will exists, when improved technology becomes available.

"Wow, Ted, it seems that conclusions of science are not final," Hank noted rather loudly.

Ted's facial expression seemed to show a little satisfaction from Hank's remarks, but he went on reading from the handout. "Next, I'll give you some points of view espoused by a few other scientists, mostly physicists, in defense of their atheistic or agnostic positions derived from their conclusions regarding free will, suffering, evil, and a questionable existence of God."

First is a quote from David Hume. He said, speaking of God, "Is he willing to prevent evil, but not able? Then is he impotent. Is he able, but not willing? Then is he malevolent. Is he both able and willing? Whence then is evil?"[5]

"Ted, without what we've learned today," Hank broke in again, "these thought-provoking questions would be difficult to answer."

After Hank's observation, Ted said, "Let me show you what Einstein thought. 'Einstein gave grudging acceptance to "the necessity for a beginning"[6] and, eventually, to "the presence of a superior reasoning power,"[7] but never did he accept the doctrine of a personal God.[8] Two specific obstacles blocked his way. According to his journal writings, Einstein wrestled with a deeply felt bitterness toward the clergy, priests in particular, and with his inability to resolve the paradox of God's omnipotence with man's responsibility for his choices.'"[9] (This whole paragraph is copied from *The Fingerprint of God*, Hugh Ross, 1991, p. 59.)

"Einstein apparently thought, 'If this being is omnipotent, then every occurrence, including every human action, every human thought, and every human feeling and aspiration, is also His work; how is it possible to think of holding men responsible for their deeds and thoughts before such an almighty Being? In giving out punishments and rewards, He would, to a certain extent, be passing judgment on himself. How can this be combined with the goodness and righteousness ascribed to Him.'[10]

"Seeing no solution to this paradox, Einstein, like many other powerful intellects through the centuries, ruled out the existence of a personal God.[11] To many cosmologists, including Einstein, Hoyle, and Davies, the existence of suffering, evil, and death seems incompatible with a reality of an all-powerful, all-loving Creator. These 'scourges,' they say, make sense only if an impersonal force or intelligence initiated the universe and established the mechanisms for biological evolution. The point they have missed is that God's plan, according to the Bible, is to develop eternally perfect people without disturbing free will. This plan can only be achieved by the operation of God's perfect mercy and justice through pain, suffering, and death and, most significantly, through the temptations offered by the most powerful created being."[12]

Loran, thinking out loud, said, "It seems a pity that these brilliant men have followed the thoughts of God afar off by their discoveries but don't even know that they were doing it."

Janice broke into the discussion just then by saying, "Since this is the last time we'll be meeting till next fall, let me dismiss you for hopefully a great summer holiday. Let's bow our heads as I offer a prayer for our safety during this summer."

After her prayer of dismissal, the group said their goodbyes as they left.

Summary of Science and Man's Free Will

1. There are two categories of evil with each composed of two others: (1) Moral evil: (a) Man's rebellion against God and (b) Man's inhumanity against man. (2) Natural evil: (c) Human misery caused by the disease-death environment and (d) Catastrophic events, such as earthquakes, storms, floods, etc.
2. The evil of rebellion against God first arose in the mind of Lucifer, an angel in heaven. Later, he was able to introduce his evil rebellion into the minds of one-third of the other angels and, finally, after being cast out of heaven, to mankind on earth.

3. When God created mankind, He pronounced them good. (a) God's first order of approval. (b) After mankind joined in the rebellion against God, human existence met with God's second order of approval when the Godhead decided not to destroy humans immediately. Instead, a way was introduced for any human, who desired, to receive forgiveness for their rebellion and return to allegiance to God.

4. The immediate destruction of all rebels, either angelic or human, would have been met with thoughts of self-preservation among those who had not rebelled. Their thinking would have gone like this: *We better mind our Ps and Qs, or we'll be destroyed too.*

5. These thoughts of self-preservation would have been prompted by fear of God and not from love for Him. Therefore, He had to allow all forms of evil to continue until it can be seen that it will cause self-destruction to all who cling to it. When that occurs, then God can destroy all evil without anyone being afraid of Him.

6. God can use all forms of evil to accomplish what He desires. Many examples were cited from the Old Testament.

7. God uses all forms of evil to encourage people to want to escape from this evil earthly environment. Acceptance of His offer of forgiveness changes His second order of approval of mankind back into His first.

8. All the above thinking is based upon God having given free will to His intelligent creatures, either angelic or human. If so, we must ask why would God do this if He could foresee that sometime in the future, an evil rebellion might arise. The answer, free will is the only way that intelligent beings, including God, can experience agape love.

9. Since God created all forms of life, He obviously holds the supreme position in heaven's government. Therefore, all other life forms are below Him. However, in order to maintain peace and tranquility among intelligent individuals underneath Him, God required each one to always place the other person first.

10. This rule was followed by all the angels in heaven until Lucifer, later known as Satan, decided to try to place himself above God. See Isaiah 14:12-14.

11. Modern-day scientists, which includes Will Povine, Melvin Konner, Thomas W. Clark, from an evolutionary point of view, are convinced that there is no such thing as free will. However, one scientist, namely Eddy Nahmias, favors free will from his research. Last, Einstein, Hoyle, and Davies try to support atheism from their observations of suffering, evil, and death.

Bibliography

1. Sylvester, Hugh, 1971, Arguing with God, Inter-Varsity Press, Downers Grove IL. pp. 29-42.
2. Ibid. p. 20.
3. Timothy Keller, 2008, The Reason for God, Penguin Group, New York NY. pp. 48-50.
4. Liles, George, March 1994, MD (a magazine). MD Publications, New York NY. pp. 59-64.
5. Dialogs Concerning Natural Religion, part 10 (The English Philosophers From Bacon to Mill, edited by Edwin A. Burtt [New York: The Modern Library, 1939], p.741).
6. Douglas A. Vibert, "Forty Minutes With Einstein," in Journal of the Royal Astronomical Society of Canada. 50 (1956), p. 100.
7. Barnett, Lincoln. The Universe and Dr. Einstein. (New York: William Sloane Associates, 1948), p. 106.
8. Einstein, Albert. Out of My Later Years. (New York Philosophical Library, 1950). pp. 27-28.
9. Ibid., pp. 26-30.
10. Ibid., p. 27.
11. Hugh Ross, 1991, The Fingerprint of God, Promise Publishing Co., Orange CA. p. 59.
12. Hugh Ross, 1991, The Fingerprint of God, Promise Publishing Co., Orange CA. p. 171.